M000316561

CHANGE WE MUST

DECIDING THE FUTURE OF HIGHER EDUCATION

EDITED BY

MATTHEW GOLDSTEIN

GEORGE OTTE

To Rebecca, with esteem + affection, and a sure sense that you know the joys + challenges of co-/multiple authorship. —George

RosettaBooks®

NEW YORK 2016

CHANGE WE MUST: Deciding the Future of Higher Education

RosettaBooks editions are available to the trade through Ingram distribution services,
ipage.ingramcontent.com or (844) 749-4857. For special orders, catalogues, events, or other
information, please write to production@rosettabooks.com.

First edition published 2016 by RosettaBooks
Cover and interior design by Corina Lupp

Library of Congress Control Number: 2015953401
ISBN-13: 978-0-7953-4804-4

RosettaBooks®

www.RosettaBooks.com
Printed in the United States of America

CONTENTS

Introduction:
Raising the Real Issues, Asking the Right Questions

Many tomes talk about what will happen in higher education. This is a book about what *should* happen. In fact, true to its title, it is about what *must* happen.

There is no single solution, no quick fix. Hard decisions lie ahead, and the authors here have important advice for the decision-makers. Their multiple perspectives and recommendations address problems that are themselves many and multifaceted. These are general problems without being generic. Manifesting differently within the stratified, complex sphere of American higher education—much too disjunctive to be called a system—the problems are fiscal, administrative, pedagogical, political. Their solutions mean changing hearts and minds as well as budget processes and governance, managing change and technology as well as teaching and learning.

Of the many things to consider, one thread runs through all: the welfare of the students. They think, rightly, that college education is important. That importance can be gauged in different ways, like differential incomes and employment patterns, but none is more striking than the level of student debt. At $1.2 trillion, it is, like

1

government debt, a number almost too large to reckon with. It is also the accumulated evidence of a form of striking self-sacrifice, the consequences and extent of which bear bracing testimony to the importance of a degree. They give unprecedented urgency to the problems of retention and completion, no less than those of cost. Like a new and virulent virus, the plague of debt overspreads a population that has seen nothing like it, an affliction earlier generations scarcely felt, now a blighting condition visited on this generation of students and, unless addressed, generations to come.

Can a cure be found? Can a college education be both affordable and valuable, worth all that is spent on it by the institutions, the taxpayers, and above all the students? And if such a possibility is a reachable destination, how do we get there? This is taken up by the first section of the book, which deals with the questions of what must change at the highest level, both in the business practices and in decision-making. Michael Zavelle argues that the FITS (Fannies in the Seats) business model is as antiquated as horse-drawn transportation in the automotive age: Alternative ways of delivering education, course credits, and college degrees argue for a new, or at least bifurcated, business model. Getting there entails a commitment not just to rethinking but to restructuring the operations of both labor and management in higher education—of all "industries," the one most resistant to change. Matthew Goldstein, who headed a vast multicampus system that changed greatly during his tenure, acknowledges the importance of shared governance, but he also redefines it for an era of accelerating change. Widespread consultation is more important than it has ever been, but responsibility—and accountability—must be concentrated at the top at a time when consensus is as elusive as certainty and as illusory as stability.

Decision-making is a reasoned response to change. Change itself works differently: sometimes disruptively, sometimes steadily;

sometimes as a kind of progress, sometimes as a mounting crisis. The second section considers how change in the larger world affects the core mission of teaching and learning. George Otte looks at technological change specifically, and how innovations are embraced or resisted in the world at large over time, especially within the sphere of higher education and our own moment. Cathy Davidson argues that our time calls for a new model of instruction, one that moves us beyond the outworn paradigms of prepackaged knowledge and stable hierarchies. The model of top-down information transfer is no longer valuable or viable in a world where information is so available, so variable, so *networked*: We need a new model that collaboratively synthesizes and applies information, both for higher education and the society it serves.

The next section deals with the means and modes distinguishing such new models. In no small part, this means dispelling the hype and confusion surrounding emergent innovations in teaching and learning. As Candace Thille stresses, the most important innovations are quite the opposite of mysterious: These innovations, particularly adaptive learning systems, are experimental in the best sense, based on advances in the science of learning, grounded in and guided by evidence, overseen by teams of teachers and researchers. Ray Schroeder and Vicki Cooke expand our view of the range of new tools and techniques while stressing a key commonality: They are all transformative, not just tweaks of efficiencies in instruction, but dramatic changes in the learning experience—certainly dramatic enough to give nonadopters pause.

The imperative to change is not enough. Change must be made deliberatively, effectively, decisively. Change, in short, must be managed, and that is what the last section is about. James Hilton and James DeVaney argue for a strategic approach to emergent change that is no more wait-and-see (for which there is no time) than bandwagon-jumping (which is foolhardy). It is essentially an argument for thinking past the interchangeable mission statements of institutions of higher education to what makes each distinctive and genuinely unique, because their separation by distance will collapse even as new distinctions—marketable or magnetizing ones—emerge. Jonathan Cole argues for an acknowledged responsibility stretching beyond the institutions, a new vision of support arising from a new vision of education and research as a public good, even and especially for private universities. This will require, within those institutions, a new sense of shared governance that is responsive rather than reactive, but it will also require a new sense of government support as investment rather than subsidy.

Whether higher education is being reshaped or is reshaping itself, perhaps one institution at a time, the one certainty is that the long-term result will be very different from the status quo. And no index of change will be more marked than the changing role of the faculty. The Afterword explores the ramifications of the preceding essays by asking what will become of faculty as new forms and modes of teaching, new technologies, and new structures become the norm. Will the faculty of the future be radically different in the roles they assume? Will they be disaggregated into the multiple functions teaching has assumed in an era that has taught us to think through the complexities of course design, of interaction and apprehension, of assessment? Will the growing importance of various forms of on-line education spawn a kind of free agency for faculty who are adept at employing the new modes? Will the changes confronting higher education create new opportunities for activism and redefinition for the faculty, a chance to forge their own sense of appropriate change?

Such questions point to possibilities, not predictions. What will happen with the future of higher education rests on decisions not yet made. How well informed they are, and how wise, remains to be seen. One certainty shadows them all—not a prediction, but an imperative: Change we must.

4

SECTION 1:

The Change Imperative

Institutions of higher education are notoriously resistant to change. New ideas are hatched constantly, to be sure, but conducting the business of higher education is another matter. Here the speed of thought is not the issue; the point is instead to ensure continuity, meet expectations, and preserve tradition.

If colleges or universities change their business practices and governance procedures only when they must, they truly must now: New forms of competition and new kinds of demands are changing the landscape. Costs are out of control, imposing huge burdens on those least equipped to shoulder them: the students.

Addressing the situation means finding a maneuverability our institutions lack. Like standing armies throughout history, they are equipped to fight the battles of yesteryear. As long as change was defined in terms of adding to or tweaking the curriculum or introducing some efficiencies to the scheduling of campus-based courses, change could be seen as improving the model. But a new model has already emerged. It comes on a wave of rapid change, while our institutions of higher education are all but immobilized by resistance to change.

The essays in this section—Michael Zavelle's on "The Bifurcating Higher Education Business Model" and Matthew Goldstein's on "Shared Governance and the Need for Decisive Action"—provide the largest and broadest perspective on what must happen. In brief, colleges and universities must change. Michael Zavelle, focusing on the business model, explains why. Matthew Goldstein, focusing on governance, explains how.

The Bifurcating Higher Education Business Model

Michael Zavelle

MODEL X LURKS

Technology and the application of technology dramatically shift business models over time. Looking back 40 years, IBM dominated the technology world, and the marketing phrase "No one ever got fired for buying IBM" had meaning. At that time, IBM enhanced its market presence by hosting industry-focused educational seminars on its campuses around the country, with higher education viewed as an important industry. At such sessions, the IBM seminar leader would note both that IBM was the largest educational institution in the world and that, despite the billions spent on education each year, what worked in education was poorly understood. This construct was education's equivalent of the advertising maxim "Fifty percent of all money spent on advertising is wasted; you just don't know which half." As in advertising, the efficacy of higher education business models will continue to improve as technological innovations refine and redefine the teaching–learning process.

The IBM presenter also likely noted that colleges and college students were best served if they focused on mainframe computer languages rather than on languages like BASIC. IBM focused on mainframe hardware and mainframe computer languages more so than on what was easiest for the average person to use. A planner with a limited computer background, operating on the fringes of technology, writing a macro-level higher education financial model in BASIC was receiving little support from IBM. Microsoft, Apple, and subsequent application-oriented companies like Google overtook IBM in part because they moved on from BASIC, keeping the needs of non-techies more in mind.

Today, institutions of higher education spend more billions each year without a strong sense of what works best in education. While the science of learning is more informed, teaching methodologies have not kept pace. The teaching–learning model in higher education has changed little from 40 years ago, though a bifurcation in approach is emerging, with significant implications for higher education.

The primary focus of the traditional higher education model has been on building a quality faculty and quality facilities and utilizing these resources well. In this approach, student time is valued only when earning credit hours, and technology is supplemental. This *faculty time–space constrained model* is consistent with providing a quality learning experience while setting a goal of content mastery. A "quality learning experience" is generally accepted to mean students' access to diverse thinking, diverse activities, and diverse experiences of life on campus punctuated by classes presided over by quality faculty in classrooms or lecture halls. This is Model A-1. Think of Model A-1 as a Quality Experience major and a Content Mastery minor.

A parallel approach, pioneered by for-profit colleges, is now gaining more traction throughout higher education. This evolving approach focuses primarily on students and really takes specialized space out of the equation. This *student time–space unconstrained model* is consistent with providing a cost-efficient content mastery experience less adorned with the frills of a broader learning experience. With this approach, the effective use of student time is highly valued, and technology drives the educational process. Modeling digital delivery systems requires colleges to have a good understanding of themselves in terms of *student time unconstrained by space*. This is Model X. Think of Model X as a Content Mastery major and a Quality Experience minor.

As with any major–minor combination, the balance between content mastery and quality experience encompasses a spectrum of student emphases, ranging from a nearly complete immersion in the content to focusing almost completely on the experience. Likewise, colleges will bifurcate in melding Model A-1 and Model X in many different and creative ways.

As the time-honored model, Model A-1 has the most credibility with the public. But going forward, over time, the application of ever-more-sophisticated technology, combined with the stamp of accreditation approval, will cause employers to increasingly embrace and provide credibility to Model X. Uncertainty about the integrity of Model X, particularly as implemented by the for-profit sector, has constrained its adoption. As the most estimable institutions of higher education successfully bifurcate their business approaches for mission and cost reasons, integrity issues will recede, accreditation of online programs will become routine, and employers will provide growing credibility and demand for Model X.

Today, a few colleges are well along in building or augmenting their futures around digital courses and digital delivery systems that focus foremost on content mastery. Arizona State University (ASU) is the most significant current example of a highly credible Model A-1 institution bifurcating to a Model A-1/Model X union. ASU, with more than 70 online degree programs, has integrated online education into its core mission, a necessity for effective modeling.

The nonprofit Affordable Colleges Online, as one example, ranks by affordability in each state accredited online college offerings, which may range from offering a few online courses to providing certificates and degrees at various levels. The website of Affordable Colleges Online (www.affordablecollegesonline.org) counts about

2,250 higher education institutions that offer some form of accredited online education.

The embodiment of Model A-1 are the 62 universities that form the Association of American Universities (AAU), a prestigious group of public and private research universities, of which 60 are American and two are Canadian. Of the 60 American AAU members, 17 appear in the best online colleges rankings compiled by Affordable Colleges Online; of those 17, 10 are in the top half of their state's best online colleges rankings. Of those 10 universities, seven offer an online bachelor's degree. Thus, of 60 American AAU members, seven are bifurcating toward a robust Model X while offering online programs that are ranked among the best in their states. These seven are all public institutions, and all are members of the Big 5 athletic conferences: bedrock Model A-1 institutions. As a point of reference, 33 AAU members are also Big 5 athletic conference members. While the bulk of Model X early adopters are not the most prestigious, best-known institutions, significant institutions are signing on, and college business modeling will need to adapt.

LESSONS LEARNED

One lesson learned from the IBM example is that IBM focused on building ever-more-powerful hardware while paying insufficient attention to software applications for those with minimal computer needs but with real information needs. Likewise, higher education today seems intent on building ever-more-attractive physical plants while failing to recognize that its future requires reaching students with minimal physical space needs but with real content mastery needs. Investment in high-cost, high-quality physical space, while undoubtedly improving the quality of the educational experience for those who can afford it, tends to widen the income inequality gap, as less economically advantaged students, in order to master content, are priced out of an on-campus education and into the arms of lower cost, and often lower quality, providers.

Physical facilities are not the essence of learning; mastering content is. Yet the quality of education does indeed benefit from superior facilities and proximity; the educational experience is enhanced by exposure to, and participation in, art, music, theater, and athletics; students also learn from extracurricular activities and from student interaction. When students of diverse views learn together, content is put in better context. Quality experiences are the essence of Model A-1... if one can afford Model A-1.

For more resource-constrained students, mastery of content is an attractive place to begin. Software innovations over time will improve the ability of all students to master content at home, at work, and away from campus. Once such innovations take hold, all but the most richly endowed colleges will need to complement their Model A-1 approach with Model X innovations or else risk their long-term fiscal sustainability.

The digital age will affect the basic structure of higher education in ways that the introduction of computers did not. Digital innovations increasingly allow individuals to be effectively in two or more places at the same time while more effectively selecting learning approaches best suited to their specific needs. The dramatic altering of what physical space means in higher education, combined with more targeted teaching methods, will ultimately lead to a more sustainable cost model.

COST SUSTAINABILITY

For integrated Model A-1 and Model X computer modeling to be more than a sideshow, the lack of sustainability of higher education's current faculty time-centric cost model must be accepted and embraced. William G. Bowen, in his book *Higher Education in the Digital Age*, makes the case that higher education suffers from the "cost disease":

> The basic idea is simple: in labor-intensive industries such as the performing arts and education, there is less opportunity than in other sectors to increase productivity by, for example, substituting capital for labor. Yet markets dictate that, over time, wages for comparably qualified individuals have to increase at roughly the same rate in all industries. As a result, unit labor costs must be expected to rise faster in the performing arts and education than in the economy overall. (pp. 3–4)

Higher education is a labor-intensive industry. Even models with sophisticated physical plant databases are nevertheless faculty time-centric. Existing models track what physical space is available for use to educate students and deploy faculty. Students and faculty are thought of in time terms—how many students can fit in space X during period Y, ideally with highly qualified teachers who have 12 credit hours of teaching, research, and public service available per semester. The goal is to find enough such fits of available faculty teaching time to allow students to accumulate 120 credit hours (for a bachelor's degree) to graduate within 4 to 6 years at an affordable cost for both the student and the college.

So long as higher education remains both labor intensive and constrained by the cost of physical space, costs will continue to rise faster than in other sectors of the economy. With decreasing public financial support of higher education, tuition costs will continue to trend upward, making higher education less affordable to a greater portion of the public. Digital innovations will lower the cost of physical space while encouraging more efficient use of both faculty and student time.

Bowen quotes Robert Frank of Cornell University from March 2012:

> While productivity gains have made it possible to assemble cars with only a tiny fraction of the labor that was once required, it still takes four musicians nine minutes to perform Beethoven's String Quartet No. 4 in C minor, just as it did in the 19th Century. (p. 4)

Consider this quote in the context of a model that enables individuals to enjoy the music made by the four musicians while sitting in a theater ideally constructed to optimize acoustics. The nine minutes and the four musicians may be immutable, but other cost structure components of the performance are not. As both the arts and higher education demonstrate, the costs of putting on a performance can become more economical by making back-of-the-house processes more efficient. Yet performers, as the major cost element, dominate the cost structure. Assuming that hiring less able musicians at a lower cost is not an acceptable solution, then the relative cost of highly qualified performers puts cost pressures on the entire enterprise. This is the performer (i.e., faculty) time-centric model constrained by space.

The digital age has changed this model, as pioneered by the New York Metropolitan Opera. A live audience at the Emelin Theatre in Mamaroneck, NY, can see a Met performance live, on screen, and at the same time. Capacity at the place where the performers sit is no longer a constraint. The quality of the performance in Mamaroneck will not be the same as it is live in New York City, but the feasibility of enjoying a live musical performance has been changed irrevocably, extended well beyond the bounds of the performance hall. These digital innovations will inevitably be enhanced, and the quality of the experience will improve until the difference in quality will become almost insignificant, except perhaps to connoisseurs.

If viewing a performance at the Met is the operatic equivalent of Model A-1, viewing the performance live while sitting at the Emelin is the operatic Model X.

One difference between concertgoers in an arts setting and students in higher education is that concertgoers are not expected to have learned anything specific from paying to see a concert. If a ticket buyer sleeps through the performance, society is little affected. Students pursuing a college degree pay, but they also are expected to gain measurably from their learning experience whether they are in the physical classroom or physically elsewhere. Measuring the knowledge and intellectual growth gained by students is a challenge that constrains digital innovations, as it has always constrained change within higher education. Just as understanding how individuals learn has evolved over time, so will measuring knowledge evolve.

Model A-1 and Model X are complementary. Higher education may be some years away from allowing students to be in two places for the same content mastery while ensuring the same quality outcome. But colleges are not so many years away from reaping the fiscal benefits of catering more to students who can only afford a Model X education, or who only want one, majoring in Content Mastery and minoring in Quality Experience. Colleges can remain committed to Model A-1 for students who can afford to pay for the full higher education experience and for the quality faculty that this approach attracts, but as a Model X degree gains credibility, competitive pressures will encourage Model X adoption.

MODELING

The National Center for Higher Education Management Systems (NCHEMS) at the Western Interstate Commission for Higher Education was a leader in the application of computer modeling for higher education planning.[1] The basic NCHEMS microlevel approach has remained relatively unchanged since, and higher education has had a good understanding of how much it costs to produce a student degree by major in *faculty time-oriented terms as constrained by on-campus space* for at least half a century. Model A-1 computer modeling is well established. For higher education to have a good understanding of itself for the next half century, modeling approaches must be adapted to the new time–space realities created by digital, distributed approaches to higher education.

Model A-1 and Model X require different modeling approaches and not just different accounting approaches. Modeling requires the ability to alter base assumptions with institution-wide impact to derive the most effective planning approach to best position for the future. Accounting describes the past and measures the present. Modeling anticipates future innovations that can fundamentally change how an institution functions.

Model A-1 allocates cost to a student degree based on courses taken and faculty assigned to the courses with allocations for space used, for administrative costs, and for the costs of the extras deemed beneficial for a quality higher education experience. Model A-1 is driven by marshaling students to take courses based on core faculty availability and the availability of specialized physical space, with

---

1 | The reference to the National Center for Higher Education Management Systems (NCHEMS) at the Western Interstate Commission for Higher Education (WICHE) and to the modeling systems for higher education policy makers and administrators requires some context. Though NCHEMS was based at WICHE in its early years, it has since become an independent organization. More about NCHEMS as it currently exists can be found at the "About" page on its website—http://www.nchems.org/about/index.php—and there is a useful 5-page overview of its origins and early focus on modeling higher education systems available at http://www.immagic.com/eLibrary/ARCHIVES/GENERAL/NCHEMSUS/N140126T.pdf

adjunct faculty complementing the process. Efficient use of core faculty expertise and specialized physical space while maintaining quality experience is the focus. Student time is factored into the model only as credit hours taken, enabling the calculation of a cost to produce a degree.

Model X allocates cost to a student degree based on courses taken with allocations of supporting costs, but with the emphasis on student progress tied to the availability of financial aid. This approach necessitates correlating degree progress with likelihood of degree completion tied to availability of sufficient student financial resources, including financial aid. Model X requires managing the availability of technologically mediated faculty to teach courses with greatly reduced requirements for the availability of physical space. Student degree progress is the focus. The cost of faculty time is still factored into the model, but faculty time does not drive the model.

QUALITY AND THE ON-CAMPUS EXPERIENCE

A selling point of the college experience is that learning is enhanced by time spent on campus. While teachers are an important part of the learning experience, time spent with other students of diverse backgrounds and experience enhances learning. Taken to its logical conclusion, the best college experience is a residential experience populated by highly sought professors and highly sought students. Heavily endowed, highly prestigious colleges can and do offer this experience, but those institutions able to do so are relatively few in the spectrum of higher education. Nevertheless, even such successful but high-cost models are not immune to being priced out of the market.

Take as a given that 20 students in a room with an effective teacher two or three times a week is a beneficial learning model. With a full teaching load, the professor may have four such classes and teach and reach 80 students each semester. In this simple system, 100 such professors teach 2,400 credits in a year. With 20 students in each class, 16,000 student 3-credit-hour experiences are generated. Since each student must earn 30 credit hours each year to graduate in 4 years with 120 credit hours, the 16,000 student 3-credit-hour experiences result in a student body of 533 students. If each of the 100 professors earns $100,000 ($150,000 with benefits), teaching costs of $15 million translate to tuition of $28,125 per student per year, plus room and board. If it were not for the administrative costs, the student service costs, the physical plant costs, the costs of running libraries and providing computing resources, and all the other costs of providing an enhanced learning experience, this could be an attractive price for a quality student learning experience.

The model of 20 students per class and eight classes annually per teaching load unravels somewhat in light of reality. Even in classes with 20 students, rarely are all of the students and the teacher equally engaged and connected. Part of this is teaching styles and part of this is learning styles, an emerging field of study. British anthropologist Robin Dunbar of Oxford University postulates Dunbar's number, suggesting that professors and students are not inherently wired to take advantage of multiple intimate opportunities. Dunbar's number, 150, is the suggested cognitive limit to the number of people with whom one can maintain stable social relationships. Dunbar's theory encompasses circles that include more relationships but less intimacy as the number of relationships moves outward to 150. Thus, an individual may have five really close relationships made up of best friends and kin, 20 close relationships of which the five are really close, and so on out to 150, of which those sporadic relationships on the far reaches are easily bumped by new relationships and are not all that important to the individual's well-being or personal growth. If Dunbar is on to something, then while students benefit from being around other students and faculty members, few of those relationships make a real difference, and if they are strong relationships they need not be constrained by proximity.

What this suggests is that in a classroom of 20 students and one professor repeated four times a week by a professor and five times a week by a student, professors will have a relationship worth mentioning with only some of the students. Many, if not most, of the students will not really have a relationship with the professor. In other words, the beneficial learning model as outlined above is not a given. For many students, they might as well be virtually in the ideal classroom most of the time rather than physically there all of the time.

And then there is faculty. The best faculty members rarely teach eight courses per year, as there are innumerable reasons for them to spend time out of the classroom for beneficial purposes, including research and scholarship. How to track and cost sanctioned released time as well as teaching are key components of any cost model.

MODELING HIGHER EDUCATION—FACULTY TIME

Tracking faculty time is at the core of all higher education models. Tracking is both a function of the specific activities in which a faculty member engages and the source of funding for those activities. In a simple model, a faculty member's workload may be established as the equivalent of 12 credit hours per semester. One 3-credit-hour course meets for about 3 hours each week, so a faculty member's workload is 12 hours in class plus all of the components of teaching a course: syllabus preparation, preparing lectures, grading papers and tests, having office hours, and keeping current in the field of study. If the faculty member teaches four 3-credit-hour courses or three 4-credit-hour courses, the workload requirement is met. The faculty member may receive extra workload credit for a number of reasons, including for teaching a course for many more than 20 or 25 students—a high-enrollment course. Alternatively, the faculty member teaching such a course may be assigned a teaching assistant. The workload activities of the teaching assistant are also tracked and costed.

Classifying and tracking activities that count toward workload is very important to understanding an institution's cost structure. Another key aspect is tracking the source of funding for those activities. If 25% of a faculty member's time is covered by a National Science Foundation research grant and 25% of that faculty member's time is covered by a Sloan Foundation grant, then the workload model for that professor for a semester would reflect a time allocation that is 50% restricted and 50% unrestricted.

By tracking funding using fund account principles, with all faculty workloads compiled for a department, a dean or other administrator is able to gauge the strength or vulnerability of a department's budget. If, for instance, 50% of a department's faculty time is covered by restricted funding, 80% of the faculty is tenured, and courses in the department are on average underenrolled, the department could be quite dependent on restricted sources of funding. If grants are unlikely to be renewed or to be viable in the future, the department may have a looming budget problem. If, however, the restricted funding comes mostly from endowed faculty chairs, the concerns are lessened, though the model will need to project future endowment performance.

Computer models go into great detail on all aspects of workload, including funding. The most useful financial modeling is based on a fund accounting approach that does not discount future revenue and expenditures into the current year, as does assets accounting on which financial statements and audits are based under generally accepted accounting principles.

A college's institutional research team is usually responsible for collecting information to be used in financial models. In constructing a faculty workload model, institutional research is likely to track and count only those faculty activities sanctioned as productive. For instance, institutional research will track general activities when determining a faculty member's workload, including

- classroom teaching;
- other teaching;
- sponsored research;
- unsponsored research;
- college/university administration;
- departmental administration; and
- counseling/advisement.

Activities other than teaching are classified as "released time" activities and may result in a workload credit adjustment. Examples of the many reasons faculty teaching workload credit may be adjusted include

- supervision/advisement of master's or doctoral students;
- cooperative education coordination/fieldwork training;
- clinical, internship, or student teaching supervision;
- teaching honors courses/independent study;
- teaching jumbo/oversized sections;
- activities funded by sponsored grants or contracts; and
- administration at the program, departmental, school, or college level.

A faculty member may also earn released time not tracked by institutional research and computer models. In these cases, the faculty member appears to be underutilized. If, for instance, a faculty member is given 25% unauthorized released time, then remaining time adjusted for costing purposes to account for 33% of the time. In the National Science Foundation (NSF)–Sloan example, if a faculty member were to be relieved of one course, the NSF and Sloan funding as restricted grants could still be charged for only 25% of time, so the remaining 50% might be charged as unrestricted funding to one course rather than 25% to two courses. A student taking Biology 101 in the scenario in which the professor teaching it had 50% of his cost charged to that course rather than 25% would be a more expensive student to educate than an identical student with the same course profile taking the course from a similar professor with 25% of the time allocated to the course. Detailed tracking of this sort greatly refines a computer model.

Faculty may be granted released time outside the model

- as a benefit as part of a competitive compensation package;
- as advancement of a faculty member's research and scholarship profile;
- as recognition on an individual basis for distinguished teaching, research, or service;
- for special advancement, development, or fundraising assignments;
- for special service or scholarship (e.g., editing a scholarly journal);
- for accreditation or self-study preparation work;
- for teaching at an inconvenient location or inconvenient time;
- when a scheduled course is canceled because of low enrollment; and
- for other "good of the college" reasons.

Modeling use of faculty time clearly has its complications. What is tracked and what is not will vary. With the impact of digital innovations, some off-the-books released time will become sanctioned elements of models (e.g., for teaching an experimental or new concept course). Regardless, all faculty activities will be modeled as time based. What may change is where the faculty member will teach the course, how many students may be enrolled in the course, and the type of assistance that may be available to teach the course.

Here is where important differences emerge between Model A-1 and Model X. With Model A-1, if a faculty member is not available to teach at a particular time or if the classroom is otherwise booked, the course might not be taught. With Model X, if student demand and student progress require access to a course at a particular time, a faculty member, often adjunct, will be found to teach that course online.

MODELING HIGHER EDUCATION–STUDENT TIME

Tracking students for Model A-1 is easier than tracking faculty. While students spend most of their time out of the classroom, what is tracked is course credit. Tuition payments and tuition discounts are also tracked, but tracking revenue for modeling purposes is likely to be at the macro level rather than tied to individual students. Students from similar economic backgrounds and with similar academic qualifications coming out of high school receive similar financial aid packages whether they plan to major in Economics, English, or Ecology.

As noted, each course taken by a student can be assigned a direct cost depending on the person or persons teaching the course and their workload, with all that tracked. All university activities that are not self-supporting (e.g., dormitories, food service, bookstore, other auxiliary enterprises, fee-supported student activities, athletic programs) are allocated in different ways depending on the institution but ultimately find their way to the cost of teaching a particular course. The cost of educating each individual student can be derived once all direct and indirect costs are allocated.

The cost of educating two distinct Anthropology students is not the same, though the cost in major courses may be quite similar.

The electives of one student may favor less expensive liberal arts courses, while the electives of the other student may favor more expensive science courses. The cost of an average Anthropology major can be derived, however, and this cost can be compared to the cost of the average Biology or Art major.

Given enrollment patterns in disciplines over the years, surveys of student interests, and trends of feeder courses, a fairly good computer projection model can be compiled as to the distribution of course credits a student body of a given size will generate in future years. By varying faculty workload assumptions, physical plant constraints, and average class size by discipline and factoring in inflation and wage increases, a fairly informative future cost model can be generated. The model is made more useful by overlaying revenues from net tuition, governmental support, grants and contracts, fundraising, the endowment and other investments, intellectual property holdings, and other revenue-producing ventures consistent with a university's mission. All this guides institutional planning. If expenses and revenues are not in sync, if an appropriate balance between revenues and expenses cannot be found, then the institution must rethink its approach.

Model X views student time somewhat differently. Student profiles for each degree offering are developed by correlating progress to a degree, financial aid remaining, likelihood of degree completion, and time to degree. Thus, a student 60% through a Business Administration degree with 40% of eligible financial aid remaining becomes 80% likely to complete the degree within 3 years. Student preferences through surveys are developed to determine the most effective times for courses to be offered. Taken together, these correlations predict course demand. Correlations can be modified for modeling purposes. Given projected course demand, sections are scheduled and faculty found to teach the sections. Even for the most constrained online courses—those taught in real time rather than asynchronously—instruction can be offered when students are most available rather than when space is available to a space-constrained subset.

MEASURING SPACE IN FACULTY TIME VERSUS STUDENT TIME

Current higher education computer models do have a physical space component. Criteria for categorizing space exist in detail. Rooms or labs are tracked as to use type and as to how they are equipped. Existing criteria are, however, criteria for maximizing utilization of finite physical space, as utilization is described in terms of faculty time: one professor and 20 students from 9 a.m. to 9:50 a.m. Monday, Wednesday, and Friday. When the question is asked as to how well space is being utilized on campus, the number of seats occupied versus measured capacity is the number generated. For degree-costing purposes, that number is converted to student credit hours generated, with a cost for each credit hour determined primarily by the cost of the faculty member teaching the course (dependent on the other obligations of that faculty member) and, secondarily, by cost allocation of space used. Limits on the availability of physical space and faculty time on campus determine when a faculty member is scheduled to teach. This is a Model A-1 approach.

For Model X, student needs rather than space availability or faculty time availability drive the model. A completely online course can be taken when students are available to learn rather than when a faculty member prefers to teach (and can be scheduled into a suitable physical space). The faculty member's time is still allocated to the credit hours generated, but many more credit hours can be generated when time and space are less at issue. A faculty member may be more willing to teach if the class can be taught from home rather than requiring an on-campus presence. If the learning model is asynchronous—meaning online resources are used to facilitate sharing outside the constraints of time and place among a network of people—then faculty as well as students can benefit from flexible use of time. Classes under Model X are scheduled such that the impact on moving students toward a degree is maximized rather than being driven by when physical space is available for a class.

A rough cut on Model A-1 space utilization can be generated by the Fannies in the Seats (FITS) measure.[2]

FITS is the ultimate time-centric measure, as it ignores quality of space altogether. Rather, FITS counts the number of students officially registered to take classes for every minute of the day whether the student attends or not and whether actual seats exist or not. If, in the seminar room noted above, there are 20 seats but 22 students registered for the class three times a week from 9 a.m.–9:50 a.m., then FITS assumes that somehow 22 fannies can be in that classroom for 50 minutes on Mondays, Wednesdays, and Fridays. Capacity is measured at 100% by finding the half hour during the week when the most fannies are registered to be in seats. Utilization at other times is derived by dividing FITS at those other times by the half hour with the most Fannies-in-the-Seats during the week: the 100% FITS half hour. Patterns emerge that reinforce the notion that even in highly utilized or overutilized campuses, time rather than space is the issue.

The FITS graphs for the Fall 2005 semester on page 27 provide data from 17 City University of New York (CUNY) campuses, including both 4-year colleges and 2-year colleges, giving a sense of utilization. Note that 100% FITS occurs on Thursday during the 11 a.m.–11:30 a.m. half hour and that Thursday ranks third in total FITS enrollments, behind Monday and Tuesday but ahead of Wednesday. Friday through Sunday space is readily available.

---

2 | FITS was developed and named by the author while a vice chancellor at CUNY from 2004 to 2007. CUNY Institutional Research provided the data.

The graphs suggest that when classes are taught is driven less by space available and more by the *time* most convenient for those teaching. Students at CUNY fit their own work schedules, which may include full-time jobs, around class availability to the extent they can.

In current higher education models, space is time constrained, with time defined as student and faculty availability in terms of physical presence. In emerging higher education models, time will be much less constraining and space will be much more open. Model A-1 FITS analysis, Fannies-in-the-Seats, meets Model X FITS analysis, Fannies-in-the-Skies.

NEW MODELING APPROACHES

So long as higher education planning models assume that students can be taught only by being in the actual physical location of the instructor, planning model outcomes will trend toward affordability issues for students. Without innovation, affordability issues will ultimately force all institutions to accept some compromising of best educational practices—larger class sizes, more courses taught by adjuncts and less experienced faculty members, fewer opportunities for full-time faculty to pursue research and scholarship and to develop as academics, fewer student support services, less economic diversity in the student body, and so on. Affordability has risen to the top of the issues facing higher education, indicating that game-changing innovation is overdue. Higher education institutions need to embrace a less space-constrained future and accept the digital prospect that students and faculty can be in more than one place at a time with negligible loss in the quality of content mastery outcomes. The implication is that the higher education cost model can be recalibrated, making higher education both more affordable and more convenient for students.

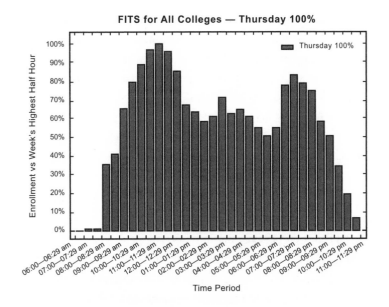

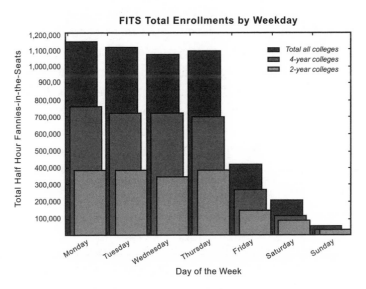

Fall 2005 enrollment data from 17 City University of New York (CUNY) campuses courtesy of CUNY Institutional Research.

As noted, the key driver in the lower cost assumption is that space added will be largely free space from the perspective of the educational institution, while the number of students focused on outcome mastery will rise. Greater affordability should result in more students served, so the model does not require a smaller or less qualified full-time faculty. Even so, embracing Model X by faculty as well as administrators will take time. Former Harvard Business School Professor George von Peterffy addressed resistance to change by both individuals and institutions circa 1970 with Von Peterffy's Law: Organizations tend to 1) secure their own survival; 2) extend their own prerogatives; and, finally, as a last resort, 3) attempt to accomplish their original mission.[3]

Affordability can be increased for students who might now find that digital innovations enable them to be physically on campus for only half the time and at much less cost without losing much in the way of educational experience through interaction with other students. Motivated students with diverse digital relationships may be willing to pay much less for even less time on campus if the means to master content hits their personal learning sweet spot. Meanwhile, the college can serve a multitude of students with a nonproportional increase in demands on or expenses for the physical plant, the administration, student services, or other on-campus services. In many ways, this is the for-profit higher education model stripped of its profit and marketing focus, producing an emphasis on student outcomes and student financial sustainability.

---

3 | The author became acquainted with Von Peterffy's Law while taking a Planning in the Business Environment (PBE) course from Professor George Von Peterffy at Harvard Business School in 1970. Any source beyond his memory of this bit of classroom content has not been found for this law, but it is worth noting that, other than Von Peterffy's Law, what content there was in the PBE course has been lost to the author, despite what was a quality learning experience.

The challenge in modeling higher education today is recognizing that space matters less and faculty matters more when both are adapted to student needs. The key to modeling in the digital age is accepting that digital innovations will result in a much better match between how content is presented and how students learn. Technology is driven by intense competition, and that competition will ultimately drive technological innovations in education that will cause the higher education business model to shift. Melding Model A-1 and Model X creatively is a better business model.

Shared Governance and the Need for Decisive Action

Matthew Goldstein

SO WHAT IS THIS THING CALLED SHARED GOVERNANCE?

The idea of shared participation in governance is hardly unique to higher education, but the term *shared governance* is most often associated with colleges and universities. It implies the participation of trustees, administration, faculty, students, and even external constituents in a process of decision-making, often leading to change.

Refining that basic definition, Henry Rosovsky (professor emeritus at Harvard, where he also served as acting president 1984–87) remarked at the 2013 Carnegie Corporation/TIME Summit on Higher Education that, in the practice of shared governance at American universities, "the trustees and president *conditionally* delegate educational policy to the faculty. That would primarily include curriculum and the initial selection of those who teach, are admitted to study, and do research." Rosovsky went on to argue rightly that universities are such complex institutions that centralized decision-making without the benefit of tapping into the "creative juices" of the talented and experienced faculty would be a mistake. He quoted Susan Hockfield (former president of MIT) to drive home the point:

> Faculty travel the frontiers of their disciplines and, from
> that vantage point, can best determine future directions
> of their fields and design curricula that bring students

to the frontier. No academic leader can chart the course
of the university's discipline independent of the faculty.

After all, who better to make judgments in shaping a curriculum
for a course in abstract algebra than a trained mathematician,
or expounding on the subtleties of quantum mechanics than a
physicist, or dissecting the structure of a Mozart or Wagner opera
than a musicologist?

Inherent in this argument is the assumption that faculties are
scrupulously careful in searching for new faculty as well as making
curricular adjustments; that, first and foremost, recommendations
to deans and provosts are backed up by the demonstration that
institutional standards were followed and upheld. My own experience supports the view that faculty do indeed take great care and
thought in curriculum development and conduct the review of
prospective faculty with rigorous reference checks, scrutiny, and
sound judgment.

But as many observers and participants have pointed out, shared
governance is complex. Gary Olson, provost at Idaho State, summed
it up as the "delicate balance" between "giving various groups of
people a share in key decision-making processes... and allowing
certain groups to exercise primary responsibility for specific areas
of decision making." That is, the process is shared; specific decisions are not. While, as Rosovsky has it, the decision to "*conditionally*
delegate*" decision-making works reasonably well, there are times (as
Rosovsky's emphasis suggests) when a less laissez-faire approach—
or even its counter, direct intervention—is warranted.

It's clear that not every action taken by a faculty member,
administrator, or trustee will be in the best interests of a university.
Faculty members may take positions largely for reasons of self-interest
or political expediency. Trustees may respond inappropriately to

pressures exerted by their appointing authority or make hasty, poorly informed decisions.

Two recent examples involved the presidents of the University of Virginia (UVA) and the University of Texas at Austin (UTA). Teresa Sullivan came to UVA as president after doing a superb job as provost of the University of Michigan. After just 2 years, some trustees became quite impatient with what they perceived as slow movement in doing more technology-enhanced learning. After being treated shabbily, Theresa Sullivan was fired, despite having strong support from faculty and students. After much *Sturm und Drang*, she was reinstated after the governor intervened. But UVA was badly damaged by this misguided campaign led by a few trustees.

William C. Powers, president of UTA, crossed swords with the governor and members of the state legislature over his reluctance to waive admission standards for some well-connected applicants. After being asked to resign and then refusing, the heat was turned up; he was given another year and then expected to leave the presidency.

Both of these experiences created high-profile unrest and discontent centered on the respective campuses. They also show how quickly things can unravel when a high-stakes game is played in the public eye. Governance is a messy business, but it is the best way we have of ensuring appropriate consultation and participatory decision-making. Removing a president is a jolting event, especially when it is done for the wrong reasons. But there will be other actions higher education will have to face that have the potential to be scarcely less disruptive. Having a strong and transparent governance structure, where boundaries are known, will be especially helpful when the hard choices have to be made. And many difficult challenges across the full spectrum of higher education are starting to be discussed more openly than ever before.

Perhaps the most egregious breach in good governance, one that required the aggressive intervention of the New York State Regents, occurred in 1996 at a small and respected private university in the town of Garden City, NY. After making some impressive academic moves, Adelphi University, under the direction of President Peter Diamandopoulos, started into a spiral of decline. Adding fodder to an already contentious campus community was the fact that he was the highest-compensated university president in the United States. There were bitter fights with the faculty unions, and enrollment fell to dangerous levels, greatly impairing Adelphi's financial health. The final straw occurred when it became known that board members were recruited by the president and given opportunities to do business with the university. Cries for his removal became so shrill that the news media stayed with the story until the State Education Department, under the direction of the Regents, took the extraordinary step of removing the full board save one member. A new board was installed, and they fired the president. This action was a black swan event but demonstrates how the boundaries of university governance sometimes need to be stretched to achieve stability and restore health to an institution.

THE NEED FOR A STRONG PARTNERSHIP WILLING TO EMBRACE CHANGE

The United States is home to 4,800 colleges and universities, with some of the finest private and public universities in the world, an array of private colleges, strong state universities with extension campuses, a large number of community colleges, and proprietary colleges. Some have strong bones: great reputations, strong balance sheets, generous alumni, impressive physical plants, and talented faculty and students. Others live precariously and will not survive as we know them today. Still others can thrive if they are reimagined by thoughtful and courageous leaders willing to take the risks required.

How to prepare these institutions for the problems of out-of-control student debt, pushback from students and parents over relentless tuition increases, and receding government support for higher education institutions is a daunting task. More undergraduates are being taught by contingent faculty today than ever before. These faculty, scrambling to make ends meet by teaching as many courses as possible, spend less time advising and working with students outside the classroom than the full-time faculty, and they certainly have less of a voice (if any) in shared governance. With the economy still in the doldrums, job prospects are not robust, leading many students to question the value and expense of a baccalaureate degree. Higher education must find ways to deliver an effective academic experience more cheaply, operate more efficiently, and give students more flexibility and support in how they learn.

So change will have to happen quickly without ripping apart the fabric that currently holds these institutions together. Good governance must play a critical role.

SHARED GOVERNANCE IN PRACTICE

Those who share governance responsibilities assume their roles in different ways. At a state university, the governor nominates and then, with the appropriate legislative body, appoints individuals to serve as trustees. At private universities, trustee selection is a more insular process, with little or no input from a governor. Faculty are recruited and appointed by their peers. Tenured faculty can be dismissed only for adequate cause; tenure, according to the American Association of University Professors, is considered a protection of academic freedom.

Perhaps the most critical role the trustees play is in the selection of the president or chancellor. The process often includes hiring a search firm and forming a committee of people connected to the university, including faculty, students, administrators, and alumni. Ultimately, candidates are vetted by the committee, and a recommendation is made to the trustees for appointment. During the interview process, it is critical that candidates hear what the committee believes are the critical challenges and opportunities for the institution. Candidates need to understand the mission and the values embedded in the culture of the campus. Clarity (and noise reduction) in such circumstances will go a long way in minimizing conflicts that inevitably arise.

With the leadership in place, trustees can spend more time with the president as they work in tandem in developing policy for the university, make appointments, oversee tenure and promotion, etc. While the trustees have numerous opportunities to interact with faculty and students, often their thinking has already been shaped by the close interaction with the president. Understanding that their time is limited and that some issues require deep reflection, trustees need to balance these realities and embrace the recommendations coming from the provost or president.

This works well when the university is perceived as creating value for the students by delivering an educational experience of reasonable cost and rigor. When dissenters both inside the institution and out have little traction in forcing a change in direction, then there is little motivation for activism.

But universities, like living entities, should shed antiquated forms and acquire new strengths that will keep them current with the changes in the world. Unlike so many other institutions in society, universities are highly asymmetrical when it comes to acquisition and liquidation. They do well at starting new things but are loath to end anything no matter how irrelevant or antiquated it has become. Some of this reluctance is about job preservation, but perhaps to a larger degree it is about a culture that just does not embrace change.

Trustees and presidents are the ones ultimately accountable for ensuring the financial health and reputations of such large and complex institutions as universities and colleges. They are the guardians of the trust we place in our institutions. When the stakes are small, mistakes and opportunities lost may be overlooked in the fog of other, more immediate concerns. But higher education is now confronting serious questions about the cost of operations, how well students are prepared to enter the workforce, what academic skills they have acquired, and how they have matured to be productive citizens. How universities effectively and formatively assess a student's progress is at too many institutions still a work in progress. Amazing, but true.

As more calls for reform resound, trustees will become more assertive, even activist, and that healthy tension with the president and faculty may upset the equilibrium that all carefully watch. But while working in harmony with other constituencies is a good thing, sometimes that delicate balance of shared governance needs to be tipped so that the institution can break bad habits and take on controversial challenges. The history of higher education in the United States is dotted with such events, and these will probably accelerate in the near future. A good candidate for challenging the way we work are those forces in play that have the potential to alter the very structure of the university as we know it today. As important as cost containment is, understanding and embracing change will better steel us for the jolts that inevitably speed up decision-making.

Perhaps most profound is how the digital environment has challenged thinking in academic content integration and delivery. Joined with the advances that scholars in neuroscience and cognitive psychology and other researchers have been making, we now have new and promising tools with the potential to radically alter how we teach students and how we assess their progress as learners. The questions that will need to be explored and the myriad paths they suggest will have important consequences for many of our academic institutions. Who teaches our students and what modalities they employ will have far-reaching ramifications by altering the models followed for hundreds of years. The big questions are whether universities can withstand the disruption and whether the process of governance will be sustainable by leading to needed change without itself being disrupted.

On matters of academic programs, no one will dispute that faculty should have a central role. They collectively have the training, skill, and experience to design courses of study, inspire and challenge students, and assess their performance over time. All of us have benefited from our exposure to great minds, gifted teachers, and prodigious scholars and researchers. So much of what we take for granted in our daily lives, from the professional people we interact with to the wondrous tools and skills we use, has a direct line back to the key influence exerted by a college or university instructor. The men and women who achieve faculty rank not only shape our skills and expand our knowledge but also commit themselves to staying current with new developments in their fields. Some lead breakthroughs that profoundly affect our lives. No argument here.

But let's take a more nuanced assessment of the faculty's role in governance. Clearly, their role is pivotal. Unlike the administration, however, where there is one president, the faculty members are spread across academic departments, divisions, and schools. And within each of these bodies, there are separate governing bodies, separate communities of interest. Further, there is a faculty governance group usually referred to as the senate. Senators are typically elected from the entire faculty and regularly interact with the administration and the trustees. Students often have a seat on a faculty governance group and may even be able to vote on policy matters. At some universities, the senate leadership may be given the opportunity to participate in trustee deliberations as ex officio members. The voices of faculty resound throughout the structures and levels of colleges and universities.

Stepping back for a moment, it is fair to say that faculty are drawn to their careers because of an area of study that intrigued them, one for which they demonstrated talent. They are drawn to university life to exercise that talent through research and teaching. That life does not have one monochromatic cast. It is an uneven and highly competitive landscape. It is the fortunate faculty member who lands within a truly nurturing environment that allows their full potential to be realized. Unfortunately, those who find the very best fit for their talents and interests are few. Just getting a "good" position is highly competitive and prized. Not surprisingly, a faculty member's loyalty to their discipline and to the welfare of their academic unit often trumps other and arguably larger institutional needs. Protecting local interests weighs heavily in how a faculty member reacts to changes proposed by the administration or the governing board. None of this is surprising, particularly since it is played out regularly across universities.

Large and sweeping proposals that may limit overall credits to graduate, proposed changes to distribution requirements that alter the balance between required core courses and electives, loosening rigid transfer requirements among institutions, and closing departments or schools—these are just some of the changes that can happen and have happened. Not unexpectedly, there were negative reactions to such steps: Students will be compromised with a watered-down curriculum, say some who take the rigidity for rigor, while others say students will lose opportunities even though the evidence is that fewer and fewer are making the choices that sustained those departments or schools. Some truly believe such criticisms, but others admit that often the collective opposition is rooted in fears about diminished resources, reduced "clout," and, ultimately, loss of jobs.

Herein lies a fundamental conflict of governance shared among trustees, the president, and the faculty: Unlike the case when an institution is prospering, with less propensity for conflicts over resources, a university facing serious financial pressures quickly finds that the cooperative spirit of working for the benefit of the entire organization is replaced by competing layers of self-interest. We should not be surprised by such behavior. We see this every day in the workings of government. The difference is that when government fails, there is a collective responsibility, and voters will respond accordingly. At a university, it is the board of trustees and/or the president for whom the bell tolls. When all the voices are heard, someone has to make the final decisions and be held accountable for the consequences. At a university, it is the president, unless it is found that the president is made a scapegoat by the trustees, as happened at UVA.

As a result of continuing financial pressures, especially at some state universities and poorly resourced small private colleges, we are seeing more stress on governance. Reductions in government support, overdependence on tuition, and not enough pressure to reduce spending have reverberations across higher education, above all in these sectors.

Things get particularly testy when unions representing faculty join forces with faculty senates to provide a united front opposing institutional change. The whole balance of governance becomes confused when a senate, whose main function is deliberating academic matters, gets confounded with a union whose focus is the working conditions of the faculty. So, with forces descending upon universities to alter course, and with the stakes so high, governance is going to be tested in ways not experienced before. Trustees and administrators are pressured by government and employers to be more accountable in how they manage finances, even as they are also held accountable in how well their graduates are educated and prepared for the jobs that need filling. Faculty can feel dispirited, and rightly so, by decreasing numbers in their full-time ranks, while contingent faculty can barely make enough to support their basic needs. Even as such evidence of cost containment mounts, students lament—again, rightly—that tuition costs are too high, even as they look out on an economy that is not expanding so as to offer more good jobs, needed more than ever to help retire the debt accrued from 4 to 6 years of baccalaureate study. These trends need to be addressed by institutional change, even as they fuel fear of such change.

UNIVERSITIES IN A TIME OF CHANGE

As *The Economist* noted in an article on higher education with the provocative title "Creative Destruction," it is going to take some powerful shock waves to disrupt a culture that "has changed little since Aristotle taught at the Athenian Lyceum: young students still gather at an appointed time and place to listen to the wisdom of scholars." Those shock waves have been developing, slowly at first, but today they are being absorbed into the mindsets of decision-makers as they confront serious financial realities. In fact, reputable analysts studying higher education see the shutting down of weaker and smaller institutions as imminent. "What we're concerned about is the death spiral," said Susan Fitzgerald, an analyst at Moody's Investors Service, using a phrase that justifies the title of the article she's quoted in ("Small U.S. Colleges Battle Death Spiral as Enrollment Drops"). "We will see more closures than in the past." Clayton Christenson of the Harvard Business School went so far as to predict, in early 2013, that "15 years from now more than half of U.S. universities may be in bankruptcy."

I want to believe that these dire forecasts are overstated; we will see. Nonetheless, the process needed to forestall them will in part depend on how effective governance can be in heading off foreseen disasters. After many decades of growth, universities are about to enter a new phase of challenges never before encountered. There will be a tendency to rely on the lessons and models of the past. If so, this will be a big mistake. As President John Fitzgerald Kennedy observed in his 1963 address on a divided Germany, arguing for a reunited Europe, "Change is the law of life. And those who look only to the past or the present are certain to miss the future." What is needed is a rethinking of how to operate a university that will address the challenges of

- controlling out-of-control costs;
- reimagining how students engage with the university;
- freeing instruction from lockstep learning that requires set schedules of time and place;
- redressing the "star system" for recruiting professors, especially to bolster weak departments;
- overcoming barriers preventing students from exploring alternatives to learning and credentialing outside the domain of rigid curricula; and
- capitalizing on the great advances in digital learning and assessment instruments.

This is not by any means a prescription for all institutions or for all students. But there are providers in sufficient number that will have to address weighty challenges if they are to remain viable. And address them they must, all the while understanding that their work has the potential to create deep fissures across their institutions. Again, it is critical that a good working governance structure is in place for any chance of renewal.

So higher education faces daunting prospects: a funding crisis brought on in part by government's withdrawal of financial support from prior levels; increases in operating support consistently exceeding inflation; demands on students asked to fill gaps with higher tuition costs; competition from less expensive content delivery; overbuilt and underutilized campus buildings requiring higher and higher maintenance costs; mandates from business and government to assess progress in programs; competition from foreign providers; and the need to ready more students in ways consistent with the needs of employers.

How will universities most vulnerable to these forces remain viable without diluting their instruction? Not a simple question, but the greater utilization of technology in teaching, learning, and assessment is bound to play an important role. How students are taught and how they learn, how they receive content and from whom—these are fundamental questions now being debated across most higher education institutions. And if online education or even massive open online courses (MOOCs) gravitate to a more central role in the educational experience that students receive, what are the costs, risks, and benefits? Certainly the early data suggest that while MOOCs, especially, have the potential to reach large numbers of students, even new populations and constituencies, completion rates are quite low. Educators have a sense of how to scale their offerings, but more study is required before widespread adoption is justified. Still, some results show great promise.

Professor John B. Taylor recently reported on the first online course, Econ 1, given for credit in his home department at Stanford University. In fact, at present, it is the first all-online course given at Stanford for credit. Working with a recording studio at Stanford that helped embed graphs, videos, and illustrations into his lectures along with study materials utilizing Stanford's online platform, similar to MOOC platforms at Coursera and Udacity, he developed

70 stand-alone lectures that have utility for different constituencies. Performance results for Stanford-enrolled undergraduates were largely the same as for his regular sections.

Great strides have been made by university scholars to form three of the leading providers of MOOCs: edX (an open-source platform started by Harvard/MIT, led by MIT Professor Anant Agarwal), Udacity (a for-profit founded by Stanford Professor Sebastian Thrun), and Coursera (a for-profit established by Stanford Professors Daphne Kohler and Andrew Ng and now headed by former Yale President Richard Levin). Early results have been mixed, but one theme is fairly consistent: When MOOCs were attempted at a number of state and private universities, there was pushback from local faculties, if not outright hostility. Some even rejected the idea without even giving it a try. One can speculate as to the reasons, but one component is fear: fear that jobs will be lost to the imported technology or that faculty will lose control over the curriculum, as instruction now comes through an outside provider.

Other naysayers have yet to be heard, in part due to the low incidence of adoption. But as demonstrated by the other essays in this volume, greater use of digital platforms for teaching and learning holds great promise for significant cost containment and better understanding of the elements that lead to successful completion of degree requirements. Over the next few years, with more applied research guiding the way, there is little doubt that serious efforts will be made in reinventing the ways universities educate their students. And technology will play a leading role. Big questions will loom as to whether there will be enough wisdom and courage among leaders to see that the best ideas take root. No doubt that battle lines will be drawn among the faculty, the administration, and the trustees. All know that change is in the air and that not confronting the challenges posed imperils us all.

GOVERNANCE IN RESPONSE TO CHANGE

What will be tested is a system of shared governance that has largely been unaltered, even during times of unprecedented growth. Higher education institutions have grown in size and complexity at a staggering rate. In the 20th century, investments by government, in particular, allowed universities to expand and prosper. With the rapid rise in access, higher education became more democratized, resulting in more participation from demographic groups that previously had limited opportunities for college degrees. State-supported institutions and small private colleges grew rapidly to address the pent-up demand. Faculty growth accommodated not just more enrollments but also new programs, and it seemed that such growth could continue unabated. All interests were well fed. This gilded age started to tarnish when other demands for a greater piece of the tax dollar became more pronounced. Governance at universities started to experience strains: It is, after all, easier to say yes than to say no. But now the tides of funding and growth are receding, and universities are being forced to operate with fewer resources. With notable exceptions, most are responding slowly.

Finding the way will take different approaches, but the one commonality will be to tilt in favor of stronger trustee activism and sharpened accountability for the president and the administration. Ironically, this may also mean that many faculty will feel more protected from intimidation and reprisals from those at risk during the institutional shifts that will likely result. The trustees and president have to be prepared for the hostile reactions to the hard choices they will have to make if the prognosticators are even partially correct. As a process unfolds, trustees and administrators need to engage with their faculties, students, and others, since great institutional realignments need many voices heard.

45

Looking at the full spectrum of colleges and universities, the strong ones with proven reputations—not just high price tags but constituencies well served and willing to continue paying for that particular brand—will likely remain relatively free from disruptive forces; the very weak, who always operated on the edge, may in time disappear. But it is the well-populated center that educates the most students and needs the most attention. These institutions are the ones that have limited capacity to reach beyond affordable tuition and government funding to support their operations.

Government cannot step up to supporting levels of yesterday, although it can certainly do more than has been the case for several decades. Capital construction has had more generous attention, probably because it is an acknowledged economic stimulus. New buildings enhance pride throughout a campus, and those that provide the academic necessities are vital. They also give occasions for local politicians to visibly demonstrate their efforts on behalf of constituents. But too many facilities are designed and built with the best of intentions but an eye to the past, not anticipating the changing mores, needs, or likelihood that communities will gather less in those physical spaces and more on digital platforms. The edifices built with brick and mortar too often are underutilized and add yet another layer to the economic strains of growth.

Given that government support and tuition alone cannot be the primary fuel at many institutions (the weakened middle and below), are there ways for these institutions to find a little relief until they get a better handle on their affairs? The answer is yes. It has been estimated that the current billionaires in the United States have a collective net worth of over $2 trillion. Many have pledged their intentions to give their vast fortunes to better society. These are highly intelligent men and women who, over time, have developed well-honed skills in making money and investing well. Will they see saving or strengthening numbers of vulnerable colleges and universities as a good investment for America? If some do, then, with the proper restrictions and justifications, this can act as a proper catalyst for change.

FINDING A WAY FORWARD

Under the best circumstances—with strong, courageous leaders; an open and committed group of shared governance partners; and recognition of the tough choices that must be made—a way forward can be found, even for the most vulnerable institutions. Central to this outcome is a healthy shared decision-making process committed to positive disruption: an openness to change that is also a responsible acceptance of accountability and long-term planning. Disruption here does not mean weakening, but strengthening. Taking intelligent and informed risks based on an honest process of engagement with the best minds on campus and off remains the best hope for a vibrant future.

TAKEAWAYS

- The conditional delegation to faculty of matters of educational programs and policy has been the bedrock on which university governance rests.
- Shared governance is the delicate balance between general participation and the granting to certain groups of primary decision-making responsibility for specific areas. The process is shared, but the specific decisions are not.
- As more calls for reforming higher education gain traction, trustees will become more assertive, and the healthy tension with the president and faculty may well tip into disequilibrium.

- Things get testy when faculty unions join forces with faculty senates in a unified front opposing institutional initiatives. Governance gets muddled when deliberating academic matters is confounded with protecting the welfare and working conditions of the faculty.
- As financial concerns become more pronounced, there will be more stress placed upon what an institution can offer, and how content is offered and by whom. Faculty affiliations will mean loyalties are to smaller academic units rather than to larger institutional demands.
- Exogenous factors as well as internal imperatives will create shock waves, requiring universities to take risks in utilizing disruptive technologies. Not doing so will result in lost opportunities not easily recovered.
- Today's digital tools for delivering content and assessing learning are still very much in their infancy. Advances will result in these disruptive tools entering the mainstream of higher education.

Key Conclusions | The Change Imperative

From vantage points rarely shared, the authors in this section have disclosed the mechanisms that have paved—and paid—the way for our institutions of higher education, showing how resistant these are to significant change. But change is a do-or-die proposition for many in the near future, so these authors show what must be changed and how change must be effected.

Michael Zavelle guides us to the fork in the road, and Matthew Goldstein notes that taking new paths requires speed, decisiveness, and accountability. Neither suggests there is just one way to go; both urge the adoption of the new but not the exclusion of the old. This opens onto more complexity, not less, and so distilling either argument down to a few key points is reductive, if useful.

MICHAEL ZAVELLE'S KEY CONCLUSIONS:

- The current focus on quality in education is less on education itself than on the accoutrements of it: status and reputations, campus contexts for interaction, classrooms and facilities. The actual quality of education itself is an enigma, confounded with the campus experience. (This is Model A-1.)
- Online instruction inverts the model: It is all about student needs and outcomes, free from the time and space constraints of campus-based instruction. This is less what we think of college life as like, but it does—or at least can—get the job done. (This is Model X.)
- Confronted with the two models, some may see an either/or dichotomy, but the recommendation is a melding of the

two. Universities should do both, each logically enriching the other.

MATTHEW GOLDSTEIN'S KEY CONCLUSIONS:

- What shared governance shares is participation and consultation but not, finally, decision-making responsibility. The buck must stop somewhere. With decisions about new modes and models in a time of rapid change, that place where the buck stops is likely to be with the top administrator.
- We must understand why constituent groups react the way they do—why trustees are likely to be interventionist, for example, or faculty resistant to change. Disruptions and financial concerns make for stress, and that finally must be responded to, not on behalf of any constituent group, but on behalf of the institution.
- Disruptive forces and new modes bring real risks, whether of opportunities that may be missed or changes too uncritically adopted and embraced. Leadership must truly lead, not just track trends, and must be both venturesome and cautious.

For both, so much depends on where the core mission of teaching and learning is heading. For that we have the next two sections.

SECTION 2:

The Changing World and the Changing Mission

Hard as it is, changing any institution of higher education is one thing; changing education itself is quite another. That happens more or less rapidly than institutional change because it happens for different reasons. Change in instruction is driven by those who offer it as well as those who need it and the world they need it for. Instructors are both products and purveyors of education, but they can also be change agents within it. The situation has its built-in tensions: Resistance to change has always coexisted with the will to change, to improve, to progress. And professors belong to a profession that, like so many, has its pressures to conform, but their profession is different from so many in enshrining the academic freedom to differ and diverge. Technology enters this dynamic as a catalyst, sparking both resistance and change. The question, of course, is to what end.

As his title suggests, George Otte takes the long view in "Technological Innovation in Education: What the Past Teaches, What the Present Promises," noting that this is hardly the teaching profession's first encounter with dramatic technological change; both distant and recent history suggest that such change, typically oversold as well as underestimated, can be change for the better, but that takes time and adaptation and, above all, reasons to change. In "Changing Higher Ed from the Classroom Up: How the Connected, Peer-Led Classroom Can Model Institutional Transformation," Cathy N. Davidson focuses more on the present moment and those reasons to change, especially on peer-centered approaches to teaching and learning that have the potential to change higher education from the inside out, rhyming with key changes in the world at large. Students need better learning; arguably, they themselves can be engines of its improvement.

Technological Innovation in Education: What the Past Teaches, What the Present Promises

George Otte

"REVOLUTIONS" AND "GAME CHANGERS"

Talk about technology in higher education often claims that *this* will cause a revolution or *that* will be a game changer. (See, for instance, Thomas L. Friedman's piece on massive open online courses (MOOCs) titled "Revolution Hits the Universities" or the collection titled *Game Changers: Education and Information Technologies*.) The terms should give us pause. At least in the realm of human events, revolutions usually take the form of uprisings from within. When they hit (or maybe just impend on) higher education, however, they are usually disruptions from without (as Clayton Christensen has taken pains to point out). Similarly, games are circumscribed affairs, whether they happen on a board, on a screen, or in a stadium. If they are based on rules and mutual understandings—and most are—changing them is usually a long, iterative process. So "revolutions" and "game changers" actually deserve the scare quotes. They're misfit terms. The kind of change resulting from impactful innovation in education is neither sudden and internal nor gradual and regulated. But it is, presumably, significant. With significant change (not semantic hairsplitting) to consider, we need better ways of gauging it. One way may be to look to the past.

THE LAST GREAT DISRUPTION

We are at a turning point roughly analogous to what happened in the 15th century. There were 30,000 texts in Europe at its beginning and 9 million at the end because of a tech "revolution" in the middle: the advent of mass, mechanized printing. The impact on the clergy is well known: These keepers of sacred texts and traditions were anxious about an unmediated transmission of these to the laity. And rightly so: The Reformation as it played out is unimaginable without the printing press, though that innovation was still fairly new and unassimilated.

Those who taught in the universities of the time also felt threatened—potentially automated out of existence by the printing press, as it were. (Let's say you were an expert on Aristotle back then; what would it mean if Aristotle himself could "speak" to your students? What need then for you to tell them what he said?) The perceived threat was not baseless, but it was rooted in an understandable inability to see how teaching practice would change—how, arguably, access to texts would force it to change. Transmission of what was said was not the be-all and end-all of teaching, as it turned out. It was not enough to know what Aristotle said; one should also understand and interpret and apply that, something teachers could help with (and books allowed them to focus on more). Practice changed over time, and changed so thoroughly that we have moved from a professoriate that could not imagine surviving the mass-produced text to one that can't imagine surviving without it. The apparent threat was a boon, like the VCR, then the DVD, and now streaming or downloadable video to the movie industry.

There are important differences between then and now, of course. What good were mass-produced texts without mass literacy? How important was college or university learning anyway, and just what was it good for? Even in this country, in the "New World," the first colleges and universities came into being primarily to turn out preachers and teachers, the same literate elite that had bristled at the advent of mass printing. The rise of the reading public and a restructured economy had to help define the ultimate impact. That took centuries and another revolution (the industrial, with the rise of the bourgeoisie and a managerial class). In fact, of all the differences, the most important is the time this took. The key difference between then and now is the rate of change.

Still, let's assume that this accelerated rate is also fundamentally a matter of degree. What are the important principles then and now? One is that technological change is not the same as behavioral change, nor is it a clear determinant of that, particularly in terms of what the potential of an innovation seems to be at the time. Another is that we are not talking about simple causes and effects but interactions of whole systems: economic systems, educational systems, cultural systems. These have their own differential rates of change, their own affordances and resistances. The outcomes of their interactions with technological change and one another are unpredictable, even if it seems, with hindsight, that those outcomes might have been foreseen by those in the throes of early change and adoption.

Differential rates of change are key here. To put it too simply, technology, if it is a game changer, changes the possibilities of the game, but not the players, or the arena, or the feelings of long-time aficionados about how it should be played. Those may change slowly, even resisting the technological intrusion. Such resistance to change has long been with us. When Socrates inveighed against writing in Plato's *Phaedrus* (because it would weaken our ability to remember), he noted that he was rehearsing objections raised by the ancient Egyptians, ancient even to him. Even then, and especially now, change shouldn't be confused with progress, at least in some purely linear and wholly positive sense. We are speaking instead of accommodations and trade-offs, a calculus of gain and loss.

What's more, if technology moves us forward, it still leaves us *us*. If technology were to make us better, we would have to *become* better, and technology may not have the virtue to make that happen. We can communicate faster, for instance, and more broadly, but does that improve what gets communicated? (Does that feel like a rhetorical question?) To return to our flawed metaphors, for technology to spark a revolution would be one thing; to have that revolution make our world freer and fairer would be quite another. For it to be *that* kind of game changer, it would have to allow and even call forth better performances from us. That, at least, is the hope. How often is it realized? Returning to our historical example, the printing press certainly gave the world more books. Did it make the world more wise? And if it didn't, is that another limit on what technology can do? That's a question we'll return to.

UNINTENDED CONSEQUENCES

For now, we need to acknowledge that the situation is more complicated than we've heretofore acknowledged. It's not just that technological innovations, being subject to some slowness in adoption, take time to reach their potential. They are often not used as they were expected (even intended) to be used. Their potential turns out to be less a matter of design than discovery, even serendipity. The history of inventions is filled with such stories, from the invention of brandy nearly a millennium ago—basically, wine boiled down for easier transport—to the World Wide Web, which started as an internal communication and information management system for a research organization.

But there is nothing incomprehensible about the incompleteness of such first steps. On the contrary: What defines the launch of the new is an existing framework that also frames the understanding of possibilities. No surprise, then, that thinking of the new happens in terms of what already exists. The history of technology and its uses plays this out again and again. The radio was originally a wireless telegraph, and described as such when *McClure's Magazine* reported the successful 1899 transmission across the English Channel.[4] Its development as a broadcast medium came later. The telephone was also conceived in terms of the telegraph—originating, as Tom Standage notes in *The Victorian Internet*, as an *acoustic* telegraph, a way of getting telegraph wires to conduct sound. Perhaps most oddly, the phonograph, developed by Thomas Edison while working on that "acoustic telegraph," originated as the first answering machine, a way of capturing phone messages.[5] We call our laptops and desktops *computers* because their lineage goes back to machines designed to compute, all the way back to Charles Babbage's creation of a mechanical calculator. (Before then, computers were actually people who put together mathematical tables and thus became early victims of automation.)

What these innovations all have in common is a tendency to be seen initially as superimpositions of the new on the old. People (even inventors) consistently have trouble seeing the new as such, viewing them more as an extension of the status quo, something to

4 | A facsimile of the report on "Marconi's Wireless Telegraph" for McClure's Magazine (June 1899) is available at http://earlyradiohistory.us/1899marc.htm.

5 | In the account of the development of the tinfoil phonograph from the Thomas Edison Papers (see http://edison.rutgers.edu/tinfoil.htm), Edison found that a diaphragm he fashioned while working on his version of the telephone produced indentations from sound vibrations and realized "there's no doubt that I shall be able to store up & reproduce automatically at any future time the human voice perfectly."

be regarded and used in terms of preexisting frameworks, at least initially. Innovations are game changers only when the game itself changes. That takes changes in use, changes in behavior, changes in the larger culture.

FAST FORWARD

So how does this matter of differential change apply to us here and now? In the realm of material production, technology can effect mighty changes. In the realm of human behavior, not so much. (In speaking of changes in human behavior, note that we have to look beyond such behaviors as staring at screens or cell phones; we have to ask what technology *enables* in the realm of human endeavor, even of thought and enlightenment, and this means expecting more of technology than feats of reach and scale.) People change more slowly than technology does. Institutions change more slowly still: They are ways of preserving patterns and valuations of behavior, and they modify those incrementally, even reluctantly (if such a word can be used of institutions—and somehow it doesn't seem wrong).

It is not for nothing that so much of the important behavioral change sparked by technology, whether the printing press or the Internet, is change that first develops and makes itself felt in uses of leisure time. To return to our ur-example, the impact of the printing press was, in some real sense, impossible to gauge until it grew beyond making already extant texts more available, when it was manifested through new publications and the preferences they both cultivated and addressed. As the reading public grew, so did the supposed frivolity of what was especially popular in the circulating libraries springing up in the 1700s. Similarly, the power and reach of the Internet made itself most fully felt with the rise of social media, particularly in the first decade of this century. In such cases, we find the most significant growth in uses of the new expanding—and changing—behavior with the uses occurring in our unstructured time. Serious stuff, the world of work and especially of education, is slower to change, indisposed to depart from the well-established way of doing things.

This resistance breaks down, but that takes time. Resistance to change is by no means absolute or even very enduring, but it represents another source of calibrations on the scale of change and sets a higher bar, a need to see reasons to change. Profit is a big motivator, but so is impact. Mere reach is not that big a thing, but influence is. (Penny dreadfuls may not have changed the world; Charles Dickens, however, may well have.) Innovations have to be seen to make a difference in order, really, to make a difference.

THE LURING TEST

So what does it take to make the changes that make a difference? We have some bad answers for that, predicated on an idea that the next big thing will be "out with the old and in with the new." It usually doesn't work that way. We too often think of innovations as inventions that displace: The electric light replaces the gaslight or candle; the automobile replaces the horse and buggy. But the fact is that new inventions almost always add to the landscape without subtracting from it. That is hardly counterintuitive—it certainly fits with our experience—and yet it is easy to miss. Why? Certainly, one reason is that, as we have seen, some great changes introduced by technology are as likely to sidestep both inventors' intentions and users' expectations as they are to fulfill them. As we've seen, the radio was invented as a communication tool, and ham radio operators still exist, but it became a broadcast medium quickly and pervasively. The computer was invented to compute, and... well, you get the idea. The history of innovation is the history of strange turns, perhaps none captured better than this reflection on the evolved use of texting from its inventor, Cor Stutterheim (as quoted in an interview with Richard Wray in 2002):

> It started as a message service, allowing operators to inform all their own customers about things such as problems with the network. When we created SMS (Short Messaging Service) it was not really meant to communicate from consumer to consumer and certainly not meant to become the main channel which the younger generation would use to communicate with each other.

Who would have known that a generation would prefer texting to talking, or why? Nor are these uses a mere matter of users' whims: Social change and social pressure repeatedly come to bear on how use is channeled and defined (something compellingly documented in Danah Boyd's *It's Complicated: The Social Lives of Networked Teens*, where she says teenagers would not have used online communication so much had not curfews, parental "overscheduling," and other restrictions cut into their opportunities for face-to-face interaction).

So innovation does not carve out a space for itself (or does not just do so); we do the carving, and we need to find a space for it in our lives, along with all the other stuff. This is why, so often, an innovation does not displace existing technologies so much as find a complicated coexistence with them, maybe even one as symbiotic and parasitic as television has done with cinema (or vice versa). Innovation is more likely to confront us with a both/and choice than with an either/or choice—more likely, for instance, to give us additional possibilities for communication than to have us choose just one. Increasingly, the need is less to choose than how to deal with the multiplication of choices. Sometimes it seems that increasing options is the whole point: that, and getting all the options to converge on the user. The classic example in the past decade is the mobile phone, as it not only became more and more ubiquitous but also less and less of a phone, a handheld device that is a camera, a newsstand, an entertainment center, a library, a bulletin board, a source of directions and recommendations and other information, and—oh, yes—a phone.

This doesn't mean that we don't have choices to make, or that displacements of one technology by another don't happen over time. Look what has happened to print journalism, or the encyclopedia business, or video rental stores. If we in higher ed want to avoid the fate of the *Rocky Mountain News* or Blockbuster Video or *Encyclopedia Britannica*, we have to take the long view, dodging the hype and hysteria but making good bets and forecasts nevertheless. How do we do that?

MR. ROGERS'S NEIGHBORHOOD

Back in the 1960s, a young assistant professor of sociology took on a subject that made for an important book: *Diffusion of Innovations* (1962). These days, after five editions, Everett Rogers is most famous for giving us the term *early adopters* (his term for those on the left side of his famous bell curve of adoption, the sort of people who jump on an innovation before it becomes commonplace or widely known). But that was not nearly so valuable as his documentation of the five attributes of innovation, all of which bear on an innovation's rate of adoption. They are *relative advantage, compatibility, complexity, trialability,* and *observability.* (More or less self-explanatory, they are all accelerants of adoption except complexity, the only attribute to dampen adoption.) What's really fascinating, and useful, is that none of these attributes actually inheres in the innovation itself; they are all matters of perception, all cues to behavior. They help explain why the real genius of Alexander Graham Bell was not just inventing the telephone (he is in competition with others for that distinction), but making sure it was installed in hotels and public places across the country so people could see it in use, even try it out for themselves. For innovations that have attained a real foothold and ubiquity, from radio and television to the personal computer and the smartphone, we keep seeing that adoption travels the same arc, running through the attributes of innovation.

Our subject, however, is innovation in higher education, so let's consider some of the challenges to adoption that Rogers helps to highlight. If we think of the adopters as faculty, the attribute of relative advantage presents immediate challenges. The new and unfamiliar always does. For educators, people schooled in studies of causes and effects, marshallers of evidence, the innovation would have to be demonstrably better to show relative advantage. In other words, it would need to have established itself and shown results, and that takes time. Without proof of its worth, the main prospect it presents is *relative disadvantage*: more work and time taken to travel the learning curve.

So it goes for Rogers's other attributes. Compatibility is a similar problem for technological innovation in education: Anything hatched by thinking out of the box is going to take people out of their comfort zone, away from processes and procedures they are used to. Complexity, the great drag on adoption, is a given, especially if, in considering technological innovation, the emphasis is on the adjective. Getting past complexity in higher education is compounded by the lack of a culture of pedagogical training and professional development (a lack that distinguishes tertiary education from primary and secondary). Professors are essentially taught to teach by the professors who taught them; this lag confronts technological innovation like an immovable object confronting an irresistible force. The lack of a focus on pedagogy and professional development also creates problems for trialability and observability: Teaching innovations lack the visibility that would ease effective modeling and adoption. Teaching, often thought of as a public performance (certainly for the students involved), is also an oddly closeted activity, even isolated and isolating when it comes to interaction with colleagues. One's research is quite literally an open book, but what one does as a teacher goes on behind closed doors.

THE CALL OF THE MOOC

Hasn't this changed? Isn't instruction now so much more trialable and observable? The great reason to ask this question is also the exception that proves the rule: massive open online courses (MOOCs). Touted as the "killer app" for higher ed, hailed in headlines for "The Campus Tsunami" and "Revolution" it would effect, the MOOC essentially took shopworn pedagogy—the lecture—and made it scalable and widely available. The innovation (if it can really be called that) was really a matter of giving exponential reach to the already dreadful large lecture course. This ratcheted up the observability for faculty and trialability for students, but that wasn't necessarily a good thing. In fact, the results were predictable. Students (many not students at all but faculty, graduate students, professionals, curiosity seekers, and a pent-up line of international students hungry for American college instruction) signed up in droves—leading the *New York Times* to declare 2012 to be "The Year of the MOOC"—but then dropped away in droves. The general failure of MOOCs became a broad brush with which to paint online instruction generally. Completion rates were regularly in the single digits. Attempts to make MOOCs actually work resulted in their being much less massive, or open, or fully online, or even full-blown courses (more like digital libraries for use in courses). What MOOCs eventually taught us in higher ed is the same lesson the professoriate had once learned, half a millennium ago, in the wake of the printing press: Transmission is not instruction.

MOOCs, the hyped innovation of yesteryear, have not disappeared from the landscape so much as they have been absorbed into it, as ventures in executive education, in flipped and blended instruction, and in other established niches. The ways they would replace or transform higher education haven't happened. The Death of the University seems to have been proclaimed prematurely, which doesn't mean it won't continue to be proclaimed. After all, there's a certain frisson to "Après nous le déluge," and it's a great attention-getting device. In early 2015, for instance, Kevin Carey, long a critic of higher ed's status quo, published *The End of College* (subtitle: *Creating the Future of Learning and the University of Everywhere*), and Ryan Craig of University Ventures published *College Disrupted* (subtitle: *The Great Unbundling of Higher Education*).

But a new generation gap has allowed many to forget (or never to know) that we've been through this before. John Seely Brown and Paul Duguid began their now-classic text *The Social Life of Information* (2000) with the reflection that "the rise of the information age has brought about a good deal of 'endism'" (p. 16). Writing at the end of the 1990s, exploding the myths of upheaval that the advent of the web spawned, they created a taxonomy of prophecies of "the end" they called the six Ds: *demassification, decentralization, denationalization, despatialization, disintermediation,* and *disaggregation* (p. 22). *Disruption* could be a lucky seventh. *The Social Life of Information* explained why the Ds have not come to pass as predicted, saying much with just the title: Information, without a socialization to its uses, can't be much more than inert data; socialized by communities of practice and application, it can be transmuted into knowledge. Ever more valuable in a society and economy that turns on it, knowledge is difficult to define, communicate, disaggregate. Students go off to college less to learn something than to learn to be someone, ultimately a college-educated person. We consider that a valuable commodity without being able to pinpoint exactly how the transformation occurs or just what aspect(s) of it we value. So, at least, say Brown and Duguid in the whole chapter of *The Social Life of Information* they devote to higher education. And so they conclude:

> In looking at university change for its own sake or as an indicator of institutional change more generally, no one should underestimate the remarkable staying power of these institutions. They have been around, as we noted at the outset, for more than 1,000 years. In that time, they have survived many revolutions and may survive more yet, including the digital one. (pp. 140–141)

VIVE LA RÉSISTANCE

That's not a place to stop, but it is a place to consider changing direction. Brown and Duguid are not arguing for complacency in an argument made a decade and a half ago, but they attest to a kind of durability the passing years have borne out. The real question is less *how* universities must or should change but *why*. For all the talk about the importance online education (not MOOCs, or not just MOOCs) might have for colleges and universities, for instance, surveys of faculty attitudes show no significant warming to the new modes of instruction in over a decade. On the contrary: I. Elaine Allen and Jeff Seaman, surveying perceptions about the quality of online education over a decade, found in 2002 that not quite 60% of chief academic officers believed their faculty accepted online education. That seems to have been wishful thinking. When Allen and Seaman actually surveyed faculty in 2012, a full decade later, they found that nearly 60% felt more fear than excitement about the growth of online learning, and 66% felt it was inferior to traditional learning. Talk about not moving the needle...

What needs to be more apparent to faculty is not just the means to change instruction, but a good reason to change. Making education cheaper is hardly the rhetorical high ground, certainly not so much as making education better. What would it take to do that, or to create a greater sense that online learning could do that? If Everett Rogers's attributes of innovation are largely useful for explaining why there isn't wider adoption of change in higher ed, what sort of attributes would lead to change?

We need to talk of the efficacy of modes of learning, and in terms that transcend the old and endless arguments about comparability. (If the goal of education is to replicate the classroom experience, someone has to ask, *Who made* that *the gold standard?*) What is it we really want from teaching and learning in our colleges and universities? What are the appropriate expectations for what might be done, not just what has been done? For what is possible now, not just what has the practice been in the past?

For this, we need something that is essentially an update of Rogers, something that gives us a way to judge the value of technological innovation in terms of what educators value. In a book with the wry title *The Future of the Internet—and How to Stop It* (2008), Harvard Professor Jonathan Zittrain offers just that. Searching for a middle term between disruptive chaos of a hyper-hacked and insecure Internet (a kind of Wild West of the web) and corporatization or "appliancizing" (as he calls it) of a secure but commercially locked-down Internet, he comes up with *generativity* as the key. Zittrain's five features of generativity have a striking homology with Rogers's five attributes of innovation.

- *Leverage* (cf. Rogers's *relative advantage*) is the ability not just to do more but to do better and more easily; it grants the kind of extension of reach that is not so much scaling up as networking out, establishing meaningful connections rather than just diffusion.

- *Adaptability* (cf. Rogers's *compatibility*) signifies the kind of customizability that allows you not just to use digital tools and systems, but also to modify them to address your needs and goals; essentially, we all have access to a toolbox that also allows us to rework the tools.
- *Ease of Mastery* (cf. Rogers's *complexity*) is not really about simplicity (what about our world is simple?), but it is about using complex tools (like WYSIWYG editors or wikis or blogging tools) that are simple to use but nevertheless have complex effects and extensive reach.
- *Accessibility* (cf. Rogers's *observability*) is about having ground-floor access; there is no need for massive amounts of money, no need to be at the top of the hierarchy or to enter the initiates' circle, no need to proceed from the top down (which is good, because innovation doesn't).
- *Transferability* (cf. Rogers's *trialability*) is the great carry-over effect: What you learn and use in one field can work in another; what you create can be easily shared, as can the work you do in creating it. Collaboration, like customization, could not be easier these days. Or more important. (pp. 71–73)

If these aspects, at this level of abstraction, don't seem clearly tied to educational goals, perhaps an example will help. Let's take a familiar and widely used web-based collaborative composing tool, the wiki. Whereas students were formerly asked to do research projects individually, each laboring in isolation, a wiki allows them to work together, learning from one another, even as it tracks the precise time and extent of each person's contribution. There are no division-of-labor concerns here, nor is this just about presentation. Since information is so easily gathered, the goal is no longer (just) gathering it and presenting it, but doing something with it. For those familiar with Bloom's taxonomy, and especially Anderson and Krathwohl's updating of it for the 21st century, the idea is to move from learning as acquisition to learning as application and, ideally, evaluation and creation. For example, students in a political science class would not simply research literary and historical utopias but develop their own, and do that as a team negotiating each key point, their work on this tracked more carefully and minutely by the technology than it ever could be before, even by the most scrutinizing and interventionist instructor. Of course, why stop with one tool or mode? Why not employ gamification and critical simulation, as Francesco Crocco did recently with his course on utopias (and described in the Spring 2015 issue of the *Journal of Interactive Technology and Pedagogy*)? Why not network an assignment across multiple courses and disciplines, as Cathy Davidson's Future's Initiative has shown the way to in the "Mapping the Futures of Higher Education" metacourse she taught with William Kelly? With collaboration and intentional design, generativity grows.

BY WAY OF CONCLUSION

What is striking in such models is that instruction improves—which is to say *more is learned*—not because the individual instructor does more work, but because the students are more active and engaged, moving more quickly to applications of learning. Technology has made possible what our world has arguably always needed and now needs more than ever: modes of instruction that break with a broadcasting model of teaching to a networked communication model. Nothing could be more logical, given the tools we have. But we still have acted as if the idea was to "package" knowledge in a lecture and give that to the students, not least of all in the case of the early MOOCs. Is there really any question that what students need now is not prepackaged, but something they can be helped and guided to gather for themselves, test and apply in teams, and ultimately use to build new knowledge? Faculty are not irrelevant to this model. On the contrary, they are arguably more important than ever before, structuring the learning experience, filtering without prescribing the sources, identifying the key issues and tensions, suggesting the right elements to synthesize (and, ideally, learning from and sharing with one another as they do all this).

It is as if we are on the verge, at last, of what it had taken the profession so long to learn about what the book could and could not teach. Just as what the book "says" is insufficient, what technology provides the students is not all that they need. The socialization and structuration of the learning experience are still critical, as are the faculty who will shape that experience. In the past, the key had been to guide interpretation and build the capacity to do that for oneself. Now, with collaboration ever more important, the key may be to orchestrate how those interactions occur and what goals they are directed toward, at least until the student can conduct her own orchestrations. It is a consummation devoutly to be wished. And it is not the Death of the University, but a new life.

Changing Higher Ed From the Classroom Up: How the Connected, Peer-Led Classroom Can Model Institutional Transformation

Cathy N. Davidson

WHY PEDAGOGICAL CHANGE SHOULD LEAD INSTITUTIONAL CHANGE

Institutional change does not happen overnight. The apparatus of U.S. higher education that we have inherited took nearly 60 years to formulate and implement, and another 100 years to develop to its current state. Although higher education needs to change now, that is not likely to happen any more rapidly now than it did in the period between roughly 1865 and 1925, when educational leaders transformed the Puritan system they inherited into the modern American research university that they deemed to be relevant to the age of the steam engine, the telegraph, and the assembly line. It took decades to design the interlocking features of the specialized, standardized, professionalized, credentialed, and siloed disciplinary forms of knowledge inspired by management theories of the Industrial Age. It will take us at least that long to redesign higher education for the Age of Google. Yet the good news is that, even as we work toward institutional transformation, there is much we can do immediately, in our pedagogy, in our onsite and online teaching, to promote effective, innovative learning designed to prepare students to lead productive, fulfilling, socially responsible lives. And the even better news is that many of us are doing this already, designing engaged, active, creative new methods for teaching and learning.

In this essay, I will look at ways educators are developing interactive, collaborative pedagogies suitable for the world we live in, and how they enhance those methods by connecting with other creative educators using simple, available commercial or free open-source digital tools. Contrary to all the books and op eds decrying the dismal intransigence of higher education and college professors, thousands of college professors are exploring innovative methods, forms, theories, and research and putting them into practice in classrooms, even as we attempt to change our institutions too.[6] Rather than casting about for venture capitalists outside of higher education to "save" us from ourselves (typically with quite a high price tag), with such hyped "solutions" as massive open online courses (MOOCs), this essay looks at ways many educators are making meaningful change, from the ground up, starting in our courses. I would suggest that by using peer pedagogy and peer activism as foundational models, we can build outward from the classroom (whether onsite or online) to collective, collaborative models of institutional transformation.

PEER, CONNECTED, ACTIVE, ENGAGED, CONSTRUCTIVIST LEARNING

The method of instruction that many of us are developing to address the changing requirements of the contemporary world is variously called *peer learning, peer-to-peer learning, active learning, dialogic learning,* or *engaged learning*. More recently, the John D. and Catherine T. MacArthur Foundation's Digital Media and Learning Initiative has

---

6 | Zemsky (2013) argues that people have been calling for change and failing to change for decades but that the calls for education reform rarely focus on actual teaching and on students.

adopted the term *connected learning* to underscore the digital or technological aspect of this form of learning, which supports students in finding ways to connect their own informal (often online) interests, talents, and communities to their formal education. In this essay, I will largely be using the term peer learning as shorthand to encompass the many varieties of constructivist pedagogy that educators are adopting in response to the cognitive, epistemological, and cultural challenges and opportunities of the Internet age (Davidson & Goldberg, 2011).

Interest-driven, collaborative, project-based, experientially centered, and always with an eye toward civic or public contribution, peer learning updates thinkers such as John Dewey, Jean Piaget, and Paolo Freire for the Internet age. It is based on the assumption that we now live in an increasingly blurred and fast-changing world, where the binaries that shaped the modernist university during the Industrial Age are being compromised. What is the boundary between labor versus leisure when my mobile device puts both at my fingertips all the time? Where is the line between teacher versus student, expert versus amateur, in a world of Wikipedia, Yelp, or Ask.com? Most of us now routinely take advice from participating online peers, including anonymous strangers without demonstrated credentials, reputation, or disciplinary expertise. There has been a massive social shift in authority, in our assumptions about how we learn, how we obtain valid information, whom we trust, and what constitutes a reliable source. Instead of turning to certified experts, we all now routinely learn things online, including from anonymous strangers, and with more or less success make judgments about what is or is not credible information. Peer learning asks how we can translate those skills to formal education, improving on them to maximize opportunities and minimize dangers.

We need to develop learning skills that respond to the remarkable changes that have already taken place in online interactions.

We also need to be aware of our learning habits and practices (an awareness often called *meta-cognition*). We need more deep-level reasoning that helps us learn how to learn; how to take in feedback from others; how to adapt to new paradigms; and how to think critically, carefully, and creatively about the technologies we use (including such older technologies as books and pencils, index cards, or Post-it notes). These are all foundational goals for active, engaged peer learning pedagogies.

Peer learning sees education as intimately tied to the goals of society at large and so underscores the importance of the learner's own contribution to public knowledge and supports re-investment in higher education as a public good. By no means does peer learning preclude contemplation, introspection, theoretical speculation, critical thinking, or solitary working through of a complex idea. On the contrary, peer learning celebrates the full diversity of various ways of knowing and seeks to re-balance and re-integrate the "two cultures" division of the technological from the humanistic. C. P. Snow (1959)—a chemist who was also a novelist—famously attributed that intellectual and educational division to modernity and the scientific revolution. It is time to reunite the two cultures for the Internet revolution of our postmodern age.

PEER LEARNING IN A CONNECTED AGE

Our world changed, for all intents and purposes, on April 22, 1993. That is the day the scientists at the National Center for Supercomputing Applications, based at the University of Illinois at Urbana–Champaign, released the Mosaic 1.0 browser for commercial use. Before that, only scientists, universities, the military, and a few corporations had the ability that we now all have: to communicate anything we want to anyone else in the world who has an Internet connection. Even more significantly, there is no editor or pause

74

button to broker what content you make available. That is a challenge we've not had before as humans. It is one we have embraced to an extent no one could have anticipated.

By some estimates, Internet use increased by 250,000 times in the year following the release of the Mosaic 1.0 browser. No other invention in human history has spread as rapidly or globally as the Internet. It has changed so many of what seemed like "fixed" ways in which we interact with one another, including our ideas of public and private, our separation of leisure and work. No one could have predicted a generation ago that people would use online tools and services in just about every aspect of their lives, including offering advice, recommendations, and use of their homes, and in giving unsolicited and even anonymous feedback, including to the rich and famous (helpful or trollish).

But simply being the fastest, most globally adopted technology does not make the Internet the source of everything and anything in our cognitive, social, and work lives. A major mistake made by pundits who rail about "the Internet making us ___" (you fill in the blank: distracted, stupid, shallow, lonely, etc.) is in thinking that a major technological change that accelerates the rearrangements of everyday life *also* changes our emotions, habits, preparation, and accomplishment within those new arrangements. This is *technological determinism*, or what is sometimes called *technocratic* thinking: the idea that technology "makes us" other than we as humans are. Technocratic thinking can be technophilic (technology will solve all problems) or technophobic (technology is the cause of all problems).

Peer learning teaches us how to think through, with, and about the affordances of the technology we have inherited. The term *affordances* was coined by psychologists James J. Gibson and Eleanor Gibson (1977) to help us understand what specific tools, dispositions, or environments enable or disable. The human–computer interface theoretician Donald Norman (1988) later adapted the term affordance to describe the benefits and drawbacks of humans (with their ranges of abilities and inabilities) interacting with machines (with their ranges of abilities and inabilities). Humans have affordances (we are smart, but we cannot fly). We use tools that have specific affordances to aid us in tasks that are difficult or impossible for us (such as an airplane). Those same tools cannot help us compensate for our own limits in areas for which they were not designed. An airplane cannot solve our calculus homework (although we well might finish our calculus homework on an airplane).

Like all tools, the Internet has affordances—that is, things that it allows or enables to happen. The Internet affords us the ability to communicate anything we wish instantaneously to anyone else with an Internet connection. It does *not* afford us the ability to communicate wisely. Nor does the Internet necessarily encourage us to understand instantly the complex terms of our participation (how many "terms of use" agreements do you read thoroughly and understand?). It *could*, had it been programmed to do so. But it doesn't.

My own research into the cognitive and attentional benefits of peer learning fits within the ecology of other quantitative and qualitative research designed to address the affordances of the Internet by transforming the affordances of the Industrial Age design of modern education. I am referring to scholars such as Danah Boyd (2014), Mizuko Ito (2013), Elizabeth Losh (2014), Howard Rheingold (2012), and others who advocate a peer learning that pays particular attention to what are often called *digital literacies*. These literacies include cognitive, critical skills that we can develop to understand what is happening with our data—for example, when we send it up to what is called, all too innocently, "the cloud." Digital literacies enhance the affordances of the Internet in both directions: They supply the creative and technical skills that allow us to maximize the Internet's affordances and the critical thinking skills that allow us to consider and, where possible, minimize the potential risks. But rather than just be admonitory—a harangue or a jeremiad, the tone too frequent among technophobic pundits—peer learning insists that students learn to *practice* digital literacies, to build websites, to blog on Tumblr or Instagram, and even to learn to code to understand digital architecture in order to use it well and wisely. Peer learning helps students find the appropriate tools, methods, and partners to enable and enhance their own learning.

Peer learning is rooted in another assumption that marks a difference from either traditional hierarchical approaches or new technocratic solutions that imply that one single tool or learning management system will really transform education. A hierarchical structure implicitly and explicitly assumes that the chief asset in the room is a predefined body of content as determined by a professor whose expertise has been certified by past professors who have tested him or her and awarded the credentials to test and certify his or her students. The ultimate goal in this structure is earning the grade and then the credential, and the educational experience is structured institutionally to that goal.

Peer learning is rooted in some of the real-world, experiential learning methods characteristic of medicine, engineering, architecture, or studio art and music, where the goal is to move beyond the mastery of content to create something new—an invention, a work of art or music, a new building, or a treatment for a patient, often in a collaborative process where one learns by doing. For example, in art, music, and architectural practice, the *studio crit* or *design studio crit* is a cornerstone, with students learning early on to display their work in public and learning how to accept and build upon the feedback they receive.

Connected learning similarly underscores the importance of iteration and of learning how to learn: that is, learning how to give and receive constructive feedback, use it to take a project closer to excellence, and then use the collective analysis of one's peers to improve still further. For professors, this requires restructuring the classroom's closed unidirectional architecture into a format that allows everyone to contribute to, and take full advantage of, assets beyond those possessed, predetermined, and assessed solely by the professor.

The mutual mentoring model of peer learning has some points in common with the traditional post-medical school internship or residency model known as "See one. Do one. Teach one." Students learn not just content but also learn how to examine their own learning practices and convey their lessons learned to others (King, 2002). To the medical school mode, peer learning adds a fourth condition: "Share one." Rather than writing a final research paper read only by the professor, a goal for learning in a digital age is sharing one's skills or ideas beyond the classroom. The research suggests that this method helps students to replicate and apply what they learn in one class in other situations (De Lisi, 2002). There is also a civic dimension to this aspect of peer learning. I call it a *public contribution to knowledge*, where students evaluate the work they produce and decide which of their skills, ideas, or insights might be relevant *to others*. Thinking through how what one learns can be applied beyond the immediate classroom is a skill that will serve students in the future, sometimes even pointing to career paths they might not have anticipated.

A CLASSROOM EXPERIMENT IN PEER LEARNING

In spring 2013, I taught a small graduate seminar on 21st Century Literacies: Digital Knowledge and Digital Humanities (Twitter hashtag: #21C) with students from Duke University, the University of North Carolina, and North Carolina State University. My students ranged from a PhD student in Computer Science to an MFA student in Experimental Documentary Media Arts. As with most of the classes I've taught for the past decade, this was a peer-designed, student-led class in which we experimented with an array of online tools to collaborate on coauthored multimedia documents, coding, and design projects. When I had to be away from class for one session to attend the annual Digital Media and Learning Conference, I arranged for the students to "attend" the conference virtually, via Skype, Google Drive document sharing, and a live Twitter feed. This seemed a logical extension of our class practice and purpose. And, to my mind, it was a success.

Imagine my surprise when I returned to the physical classroom only to discover that the students had mutinied in my absence. They had met on their own and decided collectively, without my guidance, that they no longer wanted to follow the collaboratively written class constitution we had drawn up during the first class. Nor did they wish to abide by our cosigned class scope-of-work contracts.[7] In my absence, they had come up with an entirely new syllabus for our course.

This scenario is feared by many traditional educators who object to peer-learning practices. If you give students the proverbial inch, won't they always take a mile? If students lead the way, won't they lose respect for expertise and authority? Won't the result be a decline in standards? These are valid questions with a long history. At the foundation of the 19th century's compulsory, public education movement is an implicit idea that the purpose of education is to transmit an authorized body of content from teacher to student. The rationale for developing high-stakes end-of-grade summative testing is to provide external, objective measurement that content

---

7 | See Davidson et al. (2013), especially Chapter 1 and the Appendix, for a detailed analysis of how one begins a course with a collaboratively written "class constitution" and an analysis of contract grading as a peer learning practice.

has been acquired. Those concerns pervade higher education as much as they do K–12, reinforced by our emphasis on test scores (SATs on the way in to college and GREs, LSATs, or M-CATS on the way out). The unstated fear in letting students take charge is that they will aim too low, and we will have abdicated our responsibility as experts, mentors, and teachers. The implicit binaries here are the modernist ones of student versus teacher, tyro versus expert, and ignorance versus knowledge.

I hasten to add that, in the case of #21C, the binaries did not pertain. Indeed, my student uprising turned into one of the most inspiring events of my educational career. What my students had decided to do, in my absence, was take to heart the connected learning goal of the voluntary acquisition of knowledge as a public good in a democracy. Instead of writing individual research papers to be read by me, they proposed writing and publishing a book, a guide to peer-to-peer pedagogy that others might learn from. By the time I returned from the Digital Media and Learning Conference, they had used Google Docs to design a table of contents and had rebuilt the syllabus for the remaining weeks of the course around the production of this book. The students had volunteered to each write a chapter of the book on a specific topic and to lead class discussion on that topic to gain ideas and feedback for their chapter. And they made a courageous promise: If they did not deliver an entire book manuscript at the final exam time, that would constitute a failure to meet their contract for the course and so they would fail the course. In short, they set the stakes for collective, collaborative learning far higher than I (or any responsible teacher) would ever set.

I am not sure what I would have done if final exam day had rolled around and some chapters from their book had been missing or poorly executed. Fortunately, I did not have to cope with the problem because they turned in a finished manuscript, beautifully designed by one of the MFA students in the course. We hired a professional copy editor to regularize the style details and, within weeks, had published *Field Notes for 21st Century Literacies: A Guide to New Theories, Methods, and Practices for Open Peer Teaching and Learning* (Davidson et al., 2013) in an open-access format on hastac.org. They divided up responsibilities and published the final product in multiple additional formats: as an editable Google Doc, in a version that could be annotated on the popular commercial site Rap Genius, on Github (a web-based hosting service used by open-source programmers and developers), and as a physical book through Amazon's self-publishing imprint CreateSpace.com, all issued via a Creative Commons NonCommercial-ShareAlike 3.0 Unported License. They also advertised it on Facebook and designed a Twitter campaign to inform people about its availability. The project management skills they learned by carrying through their ideas to publication in this array of technical, commercial, and open spaces will serve them well in all future endeavors. By November 2014, 15 months after publication, *Field Notes for 21st Century Literacies* had some 15,900 unique visitors and had been or was planned to be adopted as a text in 2014–2015 courses at Brown, Duke, Stanford, Yale, the University of Wisconsin, Schoolcraft Community College, and the Graduate Center at The City University of New York.

Is this experiment replicable? My answer is a decisive, informed *yes*. Although students' taking it upon themselves to write a book together about peer learning was the most dramatic result I have seen in a class, I have had success with radical forms of student-led learning for over a decade now. To date, I have never had students fail to set the bar higher than I would have proposed in a conventional class. For example, in an undergraduate class, team-taught with behavioral economist Dan Ariely, on the methodologies of social science and the humanities, our final assignment was for students to take the topics of the course; do their own empirical experiments, qualitative surveys, and interpretative analyses; and then rebuild the course for the general public. They designed what they called a "SPOC" (self-paced open course) that was (as they said in one of their headings for it) "Student Led. Future Driven" (Davidson & Ariely, 2013).

Perhaps because of the frustration so many have toward standardized testing, an increasing number of educators, parents, informal learning institutions, and students themselves are embracing peer learning as an alternative pedagogical model. Most notably, for a decade now, the MacArthur Foundation has supported the Digital Media and Learning Initiative where, throughout K–12, peer-learning principles have been incorporated with success. We have found that engaged, connected learning works exceptionally well in the most disadvantaged economic and social environments.[8] In fact, in over 100 projects in 20 countries supported by Digital Media and Learning Competition grants, we have found peer learning to succeed where other programs have failed (Grant, 2014). Among the most renowned are the experiments conducted by Sugata Mitra (2013), who focuses in particular on lower caste girls in rural, regional South Asia. His Hole-in-the-Wall project places computers in "kiosks," almost like ATMs, and invites kids to learn together, without actual teachers guiding the process.[9] The results have been nothing short of inspiring,

---

8 | The MacArthur Foundation's Digital Media and Learning Initiative (n.d.) explores "how digital media are changing the way young people learn, play, socialize, and participate in civic life. The goal is to make education more powerful for all students by creating more opportunities for more youth to engage in learning that is relevant to their lives and prepares them for success in school, the workplace, and their community."

9 | The Digital Media and Learning Competitions are supported by the John D. and Catherine T. MacArthur Foundation and administered by the Humanities, Arts, Science, and Technology Alliance and Collaboratory (HASTAC; hastac.org), a network of educational innovators that I cofounded in 2002.

as documented in his TED talk on "child-driven education" (Mitra, 2010), which won the 2013 TED Prize and has been viewed more than 2 million times.

WHAT INSTITUTIONAL LEADERS CAN LEARN FROM PEER-TO-PEER PEDAGOGICAL PRACTICES

If higher education is to change institutionally and systemically, change needs to come from within, from those who have the most to gain and the most to lose: professors and, especially, students. Peer learning in the classroom, where students are given responsibility for designing and implementing class goals, can be embraced as a model of institutional change. And here is more good news: This, too, is happening. Everywhere, there are new networks, new connected courses, and new grassroots movements toward educational change, often occurring in and around the traditional structures of the university.

Certainly that is the case with the innovative learning network that I and other scholars cofounded in 2002. While we have hardly had the worldwide impact of Facebook, we now have over 13,000 registered network members in the Humanities, Arts, Science, and Technology Alliance and Collaboratory (HASTAC; hastac.org). This ad hoc project began with small gatherings at several universities—notably Duke University, the University of Washington, Stanford, and the University of California Humanities Research Institute. Then, in 2004, we came together for our first international conference at the National Science Foundation to think about an alliance across our disciplines, conjoining the academy and the worlds of online peer learners, technology innovators, and technology designers. We had no ambition other than to make a space on the Internet where anyone could contribute ideas about new ways of teaching and learning that were better suited to the iterative methods and crowdsourced affordances of the World Wide

Web. Since then, HASTAC has become one of the most trafficked, interactive, and complex academic peer-to-peer websites and social networks on the web. At this writing, the Organization of American States is working to build a Latin American version of HASTAC, primarily for educators communicating in Spanish and Portuguese.

HASTAC quickly became an alliance of those cutting-edge thinkers in all fields who thought more expansively than many of their peers about the educational transformations our world demands. The technology leaders who joined included John Seely Brown, Larry Smarr, Alan Blatecky, and other household names in the history of the Internet. These distinguished computational scientists rejected the idea that the humanities, arts, and social sciences were somehow "soft" or "inferior" to technology. Rather, they embraced the fact that the Internet provided a platform for such revolutionary new ways of being in the world that we needed a new set of digital literacies to understand its social, economic, and technical complexities. Equally, the humanists who came to the first HASTAC meeting saw technology not as "against the humanities," but as a complex new tool to use, to study, and to innovate with in the classroom and in research.

The principle that separates HASTAC from almost all other academic professional associations is peer learning. Anyone can register on the site, and anyone can contribute as long as it is respectful and relevant. An 18-year-old undergraduate can write a compelling blog and claim the attention of thousands of people. The intellectual leadership of HASTAC comes disproportionately from HASTAC Scholars, undergraduate and graduate students who have been nominated by their professors and who share their own ideas and research and also become the "eyes and ears" of their institutions, representing local ideas, events, and topics on the open hastac. org website. More than 1,000 graduate and undergraduate HASTAC Scholars have been sponsored by 197 colleges and universities from several countries, and they have sponsored a number of HASTAC Forums each year on topics including Academic Publishing in the Digital Age, Visualization and Mapping, Queer and Feminist New Media Spaces, Race After the Internet, and Democratizing Knowledge.

Beginning in 2006, HASTAC became the administrators and mentors for the Digital Media and Learning Competition supported by the John D. and Catherine T. MacArthur Foundation. Although higher education and lifelong learning have been included in some of the competitions, much of the effort crosses the gap between higher education and K–12 educators. Over the past 5 years, this competition has awarded $10 million to more than 100 projects—including games, mobile phone applications, virtual worlds, social networks, and digital badge platforms—that explore how technologies are changing the way people learn and participate in daily life.

The commitment of HASTAC to K–12 learning acknowledges a central fact that is rarely addressed by pundits: *Education reform must start with higher education.* When a college education is regarded as essential to being middle class, parents simply will not do anything that will hamper their kids' opportunities to go to college. If colleges require high test scores, then "teaching to the test" will still be embraced, even by those who know its shortcomings, with impacts on curriculum, diversity, creativity, and risk taking. Unless college changes its criteria and standards for admission, then K–12 will continue to shape itself de facto as preparation for that system. The stakes for higher education transformation, in other words, could not be higher.

WHY MOOCS ARE NOT ENOUGH

An open, peer-learning network such as HASTAC may seem on the face of it to be something like a MOOC. Both are about learning, and both occur mostly online. In fact, as a pedagogical model, the two are almost diametrically opposite. In HASTAC's open, online network, communication is many to many. Those consuming the content are also creating it. There is no top-down determination of what does or does not count as learning or about the direction learning should take. As long as members are respectful of one another and contribute content relevant to HASTAC's broad mission of "Changing the Way We Teach and Learn," anyone else can take it up.

By contrast, in a MOOC, whether sponsored by well-financed for-profit or nonprofit companies or sponsored by elite, private universities, the content is delivered, from the MOOC to the participants, in a one-to-many broadcast model. Coursera, for example, negotiates with prominent institutions to have their top professors record lectures and make the lectures available online free of charge. Interactive Internet technology is the medium for HASTAC and for MOOCs, but the pedagogical message is different. An open network provides a platform for participation; a MOOC delivers content to participants.

Writing as I am in fall 2014, it is hard to remember that the *New York Times* declared 2012 to be the Year of the MOOC. The media were saturated with hype about the "disruptive" power of MOOCs. Structurally, there is no way that replicating the most rigid model of learning could truly disrupt academe, and it didn't. Nor did MOOCs live up to the original hype as the best way to save colleges millions of dollars, bring down costs for parents, and help eliminate student loans. To date, millions of corporate and taxpayer dollars have been invested in MOOCs, but there is no evidence that any college has saved operating costs and reduced tuition because of a MOOC. Nor have MOOCs disrupted traditional higher education, except perhaps around the periphery.

Yet I am not ready to write off MOOCs. I like the entrepreneurial spirit that models an ability to admit a mistake and try a new direction. I also believe it is worthwhile for students, faculty, and administrators to work out cooperative agreements across institutions that help each become aware of its own strengths and limitations. And leveraging the strengths of different institutions for the public good has potential as a model for disturbing institutional silos and modeling institutional change.[10]

MOOCs have another potential value. They have already changed the conversation about general liberal arts education being "irrelevant." It is significant that, when college courses are offered free and conveniently, literally millions of people take them, not for vocational skills but for greater knowledge. Perhaps the single greatest benefit of MOOCs is revealing how vital deep, serious research and learning across fields are to people's lives (Selingo, 2014).

BEYOND THE MOOC

Motivated by the potential to use the MOOC structure to see if the form could be turned into a more learner-centered interactive platform, I taught what I called a *meta-MOOC* in Spring 2014 on the History and Future of Higher Education. Duke University, where I was a professor, had an agreement with Coursera, so I offered the MOOC via that platform. We supplemented the traditional MOOC structure in many ways. First, HASTAC arranged a "FutureEd" year to build out and build upon the MOOC, with more than 80 official partners at institutions around the world. Each site watched the

---

10 | MOOCs did not invent collaborative, cross-institutional course offerings. In fact, in 2006–2007, HASTAC mounted an "In/Formation Year" in which 17 universities took on shared topics for open courses, online workshops, and webinars and orchestrated an academic year of coordinated, cross-university courses and programming with a new topic each month, all available to students and the public. The courses and themes were: In Common, Innovation, Integration, Interface, In Community, Interplay, International, Infrastructure, Injustice, and Invitation.

MOOC in a face-to-face setting, often as part of a traditional course or seminar. They played off and amplified the content of the MOOC by offering their own webinars, workshops, and hackathons. The linkages went from Schoolcraft Community College to Harvard, from New York City to Otaga, New Zealand. We linked the activities across more than a dozen existing scholarly networks, such as the Coimbra Group eLearning and eTechnology, a task-force of 40 European universities. More than 20,000 students registered for the MOOC worldwide and connected outside the MOOC on a variety of social media, often in ingenious ways. For example, a group of 80 deans of students from all over the United States watched the MOOC each week and then held a weekly online "coffee hour," complete with pastries, where they discussed how the week's content might be remixed for their own local sites. A group of presidents of independent colleges did the same. Meanwhile, I taught a face-to-face course on the History and Future of Higher Education in partnership with courses on similar topics being taught at Stanford, Harvard, and UC Santa Barbara. Students in the onsite class at Duke worked as "Teaching Assistants and Wranglers" in the MOOC, finding ways to engage the MOOC participants in a variety of research activities designed for active, engaged, multicultural peer learning. One project was building a crowdsourced online collaborative timeline of educational innovation worldwide that stretched from ancient Mesopotamia to some imagined future; in another, students in my onsite class asked what it would mean to "create higher ed from scratch" and crowdsourced some 200 questions to ask about the purpose of a university. They went on to create three different model universities (with their own T-shirts even). And the face-to-face students reported on all this activity twice a week in the *Chronicle of Higher Education* (2014). Not incidentally, the core textbook used in this class that turned a

MOOC into an interactive experience was the student-created *Field Notes for 21st Century Literacies.*

To do that requires the extra kinds of efforts at peer learning that our meta-MOOC strove for. And that is happening too, although, unfortunately, the independent faculty-driven networks are not making the cover of *Time* magazine. In 2013, for example, two senior scholars in media studies, Anne Balsamo, one of HASTAC's cofounders and a dean of the School of Media Studies at New School, and Alexandra Juhasz, professor of Media Studies at Pitzer College, began FemTechNet (http://femtechnet.newschool.edu/the-network/). They countered the MOOC structure with what they called a distributed open collaborative course (DOCC). Dozens of scholars who were teaching courses on women and technology linked their syllabi, peer-to-peer activities, panels, and videos. They also mounted a Wiki-Storming group of talented technology educators who added quite literally dozens, if not hundreds, of entries about women and technology, removed prejudicial or sexist language from existing entries, and worked with Wikipedia to establish a special WikiProject Feminism to re-evaluate certain standards that were biased against women.

At The Graduate Center, City University of New York, I have been recruited to direct the Futures Initiative, a program designed to train the next generation of college professors, museum and lab directors, and others as innovators of pedagogical and institutional change. Graduate Center students teach approximately 7,700 courses (with enrollment of about 200,000 students) annually in the CUNY system. Because of this distributed teaching and learning structure, we have been able to design a program that supports graduate students who are learning the best ways of teaching diverse undergraduates.

In spring 2015, I cotaught the inaugural Futures Initiative course, Mapping the Futures of Higher Education, with the former Graduate Center president and interim chancellor of the CUNY system,

William P. Kelly. We accepted 12 graduate students earning advanced degrees in nine different fields (from chemistry to classics) who were either teaching or directing programs at nine CUNY campuses. We reached more than 350 undergraduates and designed a website that linked all the students in all the courses. Rather than a MOOC, this course combined face-to-face and online learning and enhanced it through a digital community.

Visualization of Mapping the Futures of Higher Education course by Kalle Westerling

The course explored new methods of peer learning and teaching, interdisciplinary research collaborations, experiential learning, new digital tools, and public (online) contributions to knowledge. It also addressed the role of the university in society, especially public education in the United States, in a stressed time where, nationally, we have seen declining support for public education, leading both to a student debt crisis and a professorial crisis of adjunct or contingent labor practices. The student-led, student-designed course created a space in which graduate students could share ideas about digital technologies in the classroom, innovative ways to evaluate learning, the risks and rewards of student-centered pedagogy, and the real-life challenges and barriers faced by students beyond the classroom. While some students were initially technological novices (and even skeptics), by the end of the course many saw that digital platforms could help advance their pedagogical goals. In addition, the graduate students worked all semester toward their final project, the CUNY Maps of New York (http://futures.gc.cuny.edu/maps/), a series of visualizations that illustrate what public higher education offers the public—and vice versa.

CONCLUSION: INVESTING IN THE FUTURES OF HIGHER EDUCATION

One reason institutional change is happening slowly is that it usually does. The institutional apparatus of higher education that we have inherited has been evolving since the late 19th century—hardly a sprint! But there is another reason for conservatism as well: Even those professors who recognize the need for change grow skeptical when the drum roll for change emanates so loudly from the for-profit sector, and in the aftermath of decades of systematic defunding of higher education. When the accusation that professors are "intransigent" and that higher education is "inefficient" comes after decades of declining support for public education and for government-sponsored research, it is not surprising that many academics are suspicious that the real motive behind the call for "disruption" and "change" is really the profit motive—not a concern for improving the quality of the education being delivered. Two professors in the University of California system, Christopher Newfield and Michael Meranze, have been forceful, for example, in documenting the litany of calls for change alongside the cutbacks to what Newfield (forthcoming) has dubbed "lowered education." As Aaron Bady and economist Mike Konczal (2012) note, "For every $1,000 of personal income in California, the state invested only $7.71 for higher education in 2008, about 40 percent below the $12.86 invested as late as 1980."

What can we do to ensure that higher education is not forever "lowered," to use Newfield's pointed term? First, we need to reinvest in higher education as a public good. You cannot expect a bleeding and compromised system to also be boldly inventive. We need the influx of funding into higher education that MOOCs and other for-profit ventures have experienced in recent years. Second, we need more attention to peer learning and institutional change inspired by students and educators. Third, paying attention to peer learning means working to deregulate and destandardize higher education and thereby reverse a 30-year trend toward greater bureaucracy and regimentation in the way we award credentials and certify accreditation. Fourth, while we are waiting for these enormous changes to happen (however slowly), universities, right now, can begin to invest in more "edge" programs, to use John Seely Brown's (n.d.) term, such as the ones I've described in this essay.[11] We can also begin to support those professors who successfully push ideas to their limits, inspire students, and help us all think, teach, and dream more creatively and boldly.

Institutional change may be slow. Pedagogical change can happen now, as long as institutions are willing to allow for creativity and innovation where it matters most, in onsite and online classrooms

---

11 | See also Thomas & Brown, 2011.

that embody the deep, relevant practices that make peer learning vital not just to higher education but also to the world we live in now. In giving students responsibility and agency for their own pedagogical success, now, we are supporting them not just in content acquisition but also in practicing the most valuable skills for our time. To quote John Dewey, "Cease conceiving of education as mere preparation for later life, and make of it the full meaning of the present life" (1893, p. 660). We can ask no more of higher education.

Key Conclusions | The Changing World and the Changing Mission

Change may be inevitable, but its effects are often hard to gauge. So much depends less on change itself than on responses to it. Both authors in this section note that innovation is a special sort of change, in part because it is a layering of the newly possible on the established and familiar, creating waves of actions and reactions. Resistance is key to this pattern, as are deep-rooted modes of thinking, reflecting investments and traditions in education that both reflect the larger world and struggle to keep pace with it. This does not mean, however, that radical change won't happen, or that it isn't as likely to come from within as without.

GEORGE OTTE'S KEY CONCLUSIONS:

- Patterns of adopting (or resisting) technological innovations are well established and have much more to do with perceptions and patterns of use than with the innovations themselves, rarely seen in terms of their full potential, especially at the outset.
- Realizing that full potential in education means focusing less on the technological means than on the educational ends: As long as education is seen as the transmission of information and not the socialized application of what is learned, technology can only amplify, not improve, instruction.
- Like Rogers's attributes of adoption decades earlier, Zittrain's aspects of generativity give a force and direction to educational as well as technological change: The goal is to make

learning (no less than technology) more accessible, more empowering, and more collaborative—easier to modify as well as to master, and to share as well as to get.

CATHY N. DAVIDSON'S KEY CONCLUSIONS:

- Our current educational system is the result of a slow process, fitting education to the Industrial Age; re-fitting it to the Age of the Internet will take time but is a compelling necessity.
- The leading change is pedagogical, not institutional or technological, and already in evidence: It is the use of peer (connected, constructivist) learning, learning by engaged discovery suiting the world we live in now.
- Technology can facilitate but not direct such learning, though technology does encourage the sort of inventiveness and investment higher ed needs more of. What higher ed needs less of is bureaucratic regimentation so that pedagogical change can indeed be the cutting edge, with effects that will justify the necessary investments and institutional restructuring.

Both authors believe the motives matter as much as the mechanisms in the changes to come. The next section treats the growing evidence of improved effects as well.

SECTION 3:

What the Changing Modes of Learning Are and Mean

Changes currently or prospectively impacting higher education are often described in a broad, blurred view. Without looking closely, some find it possible to ascribe almost magical powers to the engines of change, as if technology could turn pumpkins into carriages, and with as little effort as the wave of a wand. But this is possible only by a kind of willed refusal to look closely, to acknowledge that there are different kinds of teaching and learning, as well as different kinds of changes and interventions we can wreak on them with technology and other means, requiring different kinds of investments and changed practice. We have heretofore done so little to examine their causes and effects. So we need to look closely at the changing modes, to see them fully manifested in application and across the whole spectrum of possibilities they present.

In "What the Science of Learning Indicates We Should Do Differently," Candace Thille takes a close look at a specific set of research-based models, using technology to bring teaching practice and research closer together, with impressive results. Arguably, the most important thing we know about learning now is that we need to know more, and we now have the means to see and tweak and verify what works. For Ray Schroeder and Vickie Cook, this is in fact the great reason "Why New Modes Are Not New Bottles for Old Wine," as their title puts it: The new modes are genuinely transformed and transformative forms of learning, various in their applications as well as in the fields in which those occur, consistent in their direction and effects. Moving education in the direction a connected and constantly changing society has already gone, they are about constant access, continuous assessment, and competency-based credentialing.

What the Science of Learning Indicates We Should Do Differently

Candace Thille

The goal of the science of learning is to understand, predict, and explain human learning. A great deal of learning research has resulted in principles of learning that could be used to enhance education; however, the results of that research often have not translated into successful changes in teaching practice or student learning. The purpose here is to describe a model for using educational technology to shift the relationship of learning research and teaching practice in the service of improving student learning. Because providing a comprehensive review of learning research results would be well beyond the scope of a single chapter, or even a full book, what follows is a review of a limited number of theory-based instructional strategies. The focus is on how these were implemented in an educational technology project that both bridged the chasm between learning research and teaching practice and demonstrably improved student learning.

THE OPEN LEARNING INITIATIVE

The educational technology project is the Open Learning Initiative (OLI), which originated at Carnegie Mellon University in 2002 and expanded to Stanford University in 2013. The OLI is most widely known for the results of several studies that demonstrated the power of combining results from research in the science of learning with technology to address the dual challenge of increasing completion rates while reducing the cost of instruction.

In 2007, researchers at Carnegie Mellon conducted a series of *do no harm* studies using the OLI statistics course. The studies showed that students using the OLI course, as an online course with minimal instructor contact, performed as well as or better than students in traditional instructor-led classes. In 2011, a large-scale randomized control study conducted by ITHAKA, a nonprofit independent research organization under the direction of William Bowen, demonstrated the same results using the OLI statistics course outside of Carnegie Mellon—in several large public institutions (Bowen, Chingos, Lack, & Nygren, 2012).

An OLI study on accelerating student learning, conducted at Carnegie Mellon, showed that students using the OLI statistics course in a blended mode (partly online, partly in class) achieved the same or better learning outcomes as students in the traditional course in half the time, with a quarter of the instructor contact hours. In the accelerated learning study, students in the traditional/control condition attended four 50-minute classes per week for 15 weeks of instruction and for homework read a textbook and completed problem sets. Students in the accelerated condition attended two 50-minute classes per week for 8 weeks of instruction and for homework completed the OLI courseware in place of textbook and problem sets. Both groups had three in-class exams and a final exam. Students in both conditions also completed the Comprehensive Assessment of Outcomes in a First Statistics Course (CAOS) pre- and post-test (delMas, Garfield, Ooms, & Chance, 2007). Students in the accelerated condition showed significantly more learning gain from pre-test to post-test than the traditional control group (18% vs. 3%). In the retention study conducted the following academic year, which was a 3-month delay for the traditional students and a 6-month delay for the accelerated students, the students in the accelerated group again scored significantly higher on the CAOS test than students in the traditional control. The students in the accelerated group also scored higher than the traditional students on an open-ended data analysis transfer test (Lovett, Meyer, & Thille, 2008).

The better performance of the students using the OLI course in the accelerated condition is especially notable in light of a study at another university that evaluated the impact of accelerating learning without using OLI. Researchers evaluated the performance of students studying statistics over a 6-month period compared to students studying the same material over an 8-week period. All students covered the same material and had the same lectures, problem-based group meetings, and lab sessions and assignments. Students whose course lasted 6 months outperformed students in the 8-week course both on an open-ended test tapping conceptual understanding and on the final exam (Budé, Imbos, van de Wiel, & Berger, 2011). In other words, simply accelerating the learning without altering the mode of instruction is not effective.

In addition to studies evaluating the effectiveness of OLI courses in supporting student learning in formal education, a recent study looked at the contribution of student engagement in OLI course activities in reducing dropouts and supporting student learning in a massive open online course (MOOC). In 2013, elements of the OLI Psychology course were incorporated into Georgia Institute of Technology's Introduction to Psychology as a Science MOOC. The study found that the probability of dropout by students who engaged in the OLI activities versus those who did not is lower by a factor of 72%. With respect to the impact on learning, the study found that students doing more OLI activities learned more than students watching more videos or reading more pages; the positive impact on the total quiz score of student engagement with the activities was more than 6 times that of watching the MOOC videos or reading pages (Koedinger, Kim, Jia, McLaughlin, & Bier, 2015).

While the results from these and other OLI studies have been impressive, perhaps the most important outcome of the project has been the OLI model of collaborative courseware development grounded in learning research combined with data-driven progressive refinement of the courseware and the learning theory.

CHALLENGES IN THE RELATIONSHIP BETWEEN LEARNING RESEARCH AND TEACHING PRACTICE

The science of learning is an emerging interdisciplinary field comprising cognitive science, neuroscience, education, psychology, sociology, economics, and computer science. Learning researchers follow a systematic and empirical approach to achieve the goal of understanding, predicting, and explaining human learning. They first conduct research in controlled contexts, in the laboratory, to understand how people learn, and then they consider how these results can be applied in educational settings. Much of what is known about learning comes from an accumulation of evidence from multiple laboratory studies and limited follow-on studies in classrooms. There is a long history of researchers offering advice to educators, yet without a significant impact on practice.

One explanation for this lack of impact is that research results are not easily accessible to practitioners. Dense, jargon-laden academic publications are likely to be ignored by faculty outside of the psychology or education domains. Faculty members teaching in their disciplines rarely have time to conduct thorough searches for learning research results or to make thoughtful syntheses of relevant research findings to address specific learning challenges in their discipline. Research published in refereed journals typically does not provide clear, conclusive answers on most issues of practice (Short, 2000).

Over the past decade, books, reports, and articles directed at practitioners and students have attempted to address this barrier by translating results from learning research into usable guiding principles for teaching and learning (see Ambrose, Bridges, DiPietro, Lovett, & Norman, 2012; Benassi, Overson, & Hakala, 2014; Clark & Mayer, 2008; Dunlosky, Rawson, Marsh, Nathan, & Willingham, 2013; Mayer, 2011). While these guiding principles are a good start in supporting student and faculty engagement in better teaching and learning practices, the principles often do not enable instructors to identify the specific conditions under which particular strategies will enhance learning. Instructional practices that have shown evidence of effectiveness in experimental settings or in specific contexts have often not traveled effectively to new contexts.

Learning is complex. The failure of effective travel can be because the research results have been oversimplified in their translation to practice, or because the theory or model is not sufficiently robust to accommodate the complexity of the new context. In either case, the traditional linear technology transfer model, which assumes a non-problematic relationship between the research base and teaching practice, has not been optimal.

AN ALTERNATIVE MODEL FOR COURSE DEVELOPMENT AND LEARNING RESEARCH

In OLI, the interaction between learning research and course design has been shifted away from the linear technology transfer model toward a virtuous cycle of research and practice, continuously interacting with and feeding each other. The learning research conducted in support of the design of an OLI module about chemical equilibrium provides an example.

Principles of multimedia learning advise instructional designers and faculty to add relevant diagrams to text or verbal description. Many studies have demonstrated large learning gains when instruction includes both diagrams and verbal descriptions, as long as the diagrams are relevant to current instruction and exclude extraneous information (Clark & Mayer, 2003). However, principles of multimedia learning do not offer sufficient guidance to instructional designers or faculty about how to create or select diagrams that will enhance learning in a specific context. In several studies conducted for the design of an OLI chemistry module on equilibrium, researchers found that textbook-based molecular-level diagrams not only failed to show a multimedia benefit but also promoted shallow learning strategies for some learners (Davenport, Klahr, et al., 2007; Davenport, McEldoon, et al., 2007). In designing effective diagrams for the OLI chemical equilibrium activity, the research and development team identified three critical factors to be considered beyond the multimedia design principles:

1 | the specific learning objective;
2 | how the diagrams make relevant information salient; and
3 | how the learner interprets the diagram based on prior knowledge and perceptual processing.

There were two important results from this work: an equilibrium module that significantly improved learning outcomes, particularly for the lowest performing students, and a contribution to the body of learning theory suggesting how prior knowledge and the conceptual content of diagrams influences multimedia learning (Davenport & Koedinger, 2010). The collaborative development work of the domain experts (in this case, chemistry faculty) and learning scientists resulted in both improved learning outcomes and contributions to the refinement of learning theory.

OLI is based on a continuous research and development cycle: Learning research informs the design of the course, and the data collected through student use of the course fuel learning research. The OLI course activities are based on the most current findings from learning research and are designed to address real educational challenges. The OLI courses serve as vehicles for transferring knowledge from learning research into teaching practice. They also serve as ubiquitous research laboratories. Learning researchers embed experimental manipulations in the OLI courses, and the system collects interaction-level learning data sets that are mined and analyzed to create and refine learning theory. The theory-based interventions help students learn, regardless of whether the teachers or students using the course are aware that a particular theory is being used or refined.

The OLI process requires a switch from a purely individual and intuitive approach to a collaborative and evidence-based approach to designing and improving instruction. In an OLI project, faculty are not passive recipients of a new technology but rather are collaborators in cocreating the courseware. Faculty members from hundreds of different colleges and universities have participated in the creation, evaluation, and improvement of OLI courses.

Teams of faculty domain experts, learning scientists, human–computer interaction experts, and software engineers work together to develop OLI courses. The OLI design team articulates an initial set of student-centered observable learning objectives and designs the instructional environment to support students to achieve the articulated objectives. The embedded assessments and interactive activities in OLI courses are designed to provide support to students, but they have an additional purpose: They collect data. With the students' permission, the OLI system digitally records interaction-level details of student learning actions in all OLI courses and labs.

DATA COLLECTION AND USE IN OLI

The data collected from OLI courses provide a detailed record of the students' learning process, making the learning process visible and amenable to scientific study. Networked online learning environments can collect massive amounts of student interaction data; however, the insights into student learning that can be gleaned from those data are limited by the type of interaction that is observable and by the meaning of the data generated by the interaction. In designing the activities and assessments, the OLI team creates a range of tasks that structure performances, automatically collecting enough pieces of evidence that can be identified and aggregated to provide a reasonably coherent picture of the learners' knowledge state and learning process. The data generated by student interaction with OLI activities provide granular detail. Aggregating meaningful fine-grained evidence is easier than trying to break down coarse-grained evidence post hoc into potentially meaningful smaller pieces. OLI courses and data systems have been designed to yield data that can build explanatory models of a student's learning that support course improvement, instructor insight, student feedback, and the basic science of human learning.

The student learning data are organized by learning objective and skill. The course development team creates a parameterized skill model that establishes the relationships between learning objectives and their component skills, and between skills and the activities in the course that exercises those skills. The relationships in the model are many to many: Each learning objective may have one or more component skills; each skill may contribute to one or more learning objectives; each skill may be assessed by one or more steps in a task; each task step may assess one or more skills.

As part of the course design process, the course development team labels each potential step in an interactive task in the course with the learning objectives or skills that they have defined. The labels are a combination of the content of the activity and a ranking of the skill based on perceived complexity. More complex skills— those that require more practice and involve more complex cognitive processes—are ranked as more difficult. The skills are also ranked according to whether the students are expected to have low or high levels of prior knowledge related to the skill. Initially, the labels are based on an analysis of the domain and on the expert's prior teaching experience. The rankings are used to adjust baseline parameters.

The skill model that the development team has created is considered "naïve" until it has been validated by data. After students from a variety of institutions have worked through the OLI course materials, learning researchers use the data generated from student activity in the course to evaluate the fit of the model and to tune the parameters. The data are used both to refine the skill model and to indicate where the course design needs to be improved.

The OLI system also dynamically analyzes the student activity in real time against the skill model. The learning estimates are computed per skill per student and use simple algorithms with low computational overhead to allow real-time updates. When a student responds to a question or engages in an OLI activity, the system uses the skill model mapping to identify the skills related to that question or activity. The model of that student's knowledge state is updated immediately after each action.

The students' learning data collected by the OLI system are presented to the students' instructor via an instructor dashboard. The instructor dashboard provides an estimate of student learning at any given point for each learning objective in the course. The learning estimate is intended to predict the likelihood that a given student is able to demonstrate the knowledge or perform the task indicated by a given learning objective. That is, it predicts the likelihood that a given student will respond correctly to previously unseen problems or questions assessing a specific learning objective.

The information presented in the learning dashboard is different from the information available from most predictive analytic systems or learning management systems. Many systems will make predictions about which students are at risk for failure based on the data they collect, such as frequency of student log-ins or student scores on quizzes. While prediction is important, these systems do not provide sufficient information to students or faculty about what to do differently to make things better. The OLI dashboard presents instructors with an authentic measure of student learning for each learning objective. The dashboard also provides more detailed information, such as a gestalt of the entire class's learning of subobjectives, learning achieved by individual students, and which types of tasks the students are struggling with the most. The learning dashboard is based on the idea that giving students better learning support outside of class and giving faculty highly useful real-time information about their students' progress will mean that class time and instructor time can be used much more effectively.

The learning dashboard was quite effective in giving faculty insight into the status of their students' learning. Building the knowledge models that drive the dashboard, designing the representation of data to provide actionable information to students and faculty, and designing the processes to support students and faculty to use the dashboards effectively all continue to be areas of ongoing research.

THE IMPORTANCE OF RESEARCH-BASED DESIGN

In designing OLI courses, the design teams take advantage of multiple cognitive principles and research-based instructional strategies, such as priming student motivation, constructing frequent opportunities for adjustment through formative assessment, spacing and interleaving opportunities for study and practice, providing timely and targeted feedback, organizing knowledge around meaningful features and patterns, and using multiple representations to support instruction.

Learning is an active process. OLI courses provide frequent opportunities for students to learn by practicing tasks and engaging in formative assessments that target specific concepts and skills. The instructional activities in OLI courses include small amounts of expository material (text, digital images, animations, and short walk-through demonstrations) and many activities that capitalize on the computer's ability to promote interaction. Many of the courses include virtual lab environments that encourage flexible and authentic exploration. While frequent and appropriately spaced exploration and practice are essential, interactivity alone is not sufficient; the design and spacing of practice are also important.

A meta-analysis of 317 experiments in 184 articles examining the effects of spacing, lag, and interstudy interval concluded that distributing learning opportunities over time, rather than massing learning opportunities in relatively close succession (cramming), benefits long-term retention (Cepeda, Pashler, Vul, Wixted, & Rohrer, 2006). Research has shown that less frequent testing leads to massed study immediately before the test, whereas more frequent testing effectively leads to study that is distributed over time. Students will not necessarily engage in distributed study unless the situation cues them to do so. An OLI course is designed in a way that encourages distributed practice and interleaving of target concepts and types of practice.

Unlike traditional textbooks, OLI courses do not group problems together at the end of a chapter, but rather distribute activities and assessments throughout the module. Concepts and skills and ways of organizing the knowledge that are introduced early in the learning experience are revisited frequently and grow in complexity.

Although the conceptual structure of knowledge in a discipline is clear to experts, it is not to novices. The array of new ideas and unfamiliar terminology in introductory college courses tends to overwhelm students into memorizing sets of isolated facts without understanding the underlying common principles (Chi, 2005; diSessa, 1993). One primary goal of the OLI courses is for students not only to learn the many definitions, concepts, and skills but also to recognize when these are operating in the process being studied. The course introduces concepts in basic form and scaffolds the extension of the concepts to other contexts, giving students the opportunity to explicitly connect their knowledge and generalize their understanding.

Many processes in STEM fields are complex and dynamic and are not easily represented via text and static pictures. The OLI biology team developed a general-purpose simulation environment that links an underlying mathematical model to a computer animation so that the output of the mathematical model drives the details of the animation (Bajzek, Burnette, & Rule, 2006). Using this simulation environment, the observable properties of almost any biological process can be calculated in real time and then presented through a computer animation. With scientifically accurate models specified by the biologists on the OLI team, the instructional activities built within this simulation environment are scientifically authentic. The simulations allow high-fidelity depictions of complex biological processes to students at different levels, minimizing the likelihood of student misconceptions. Simulations also support students in making relevant connections among multiple representations of the same phenomenon (animations, equations, graphs, etc.). For example, in a protein–ligand binding biology simulation, the activity starts with only the animation and directs the student to identify the various molecules depicted in the animation. The activity also focuses the student's attention on the key aspects of the biological process (e.g., bound vs. free oxygen molecules).

Focusing students' attention is critical to helping them learn from animations and simulations because, although it is obvious to experts, students often do not know what to look for in a dynamic visualization. Expertise depends on the ability to see features that beginners do not normally notice or recognize as important. While the behavior of the molecules in the animation is scientifically accurate, the animation depicts fewer molecules than would be involved in a normal biological system. At an early stage in a student's learning, more detail would not lead to more learning but rather would distract from the key features to which the student should be attending. As additional representations of the process are introduced (the changing values in the equations and graphs), the animation is paused, and the student's attention is directed to each of the representations and connections between the representations and the biological process. As the activity progresses, students are exposed to more complex concepts and relationships. For more advanced students, simple instructions are de-emphasized in favor of those that involve recognizing, applying, and synthesizing concepts in new situations. At the point in the simulation when the number of ligand molecules is increased, the students are encouraged to reflect on what is happening and predict how the system will react. The students write their predictions prior to running the simulation in the altered state, and their answers are recorded. The students receive feedback on their predictions both through observing the simulation and through reading the system-generated explanation. As students run the simulations, the system directly assesses the knowledge state of the learner with respect to the learning goal and provides context-specific feedback to help students refine their understanding.

The biology simulator is just one example of a learning activity that helps students learn complex processes. Throughout the courses, learners engage in challenging tasks with supportive guidance and feedback. Feedback is information derived from student activities that is used to influence or modify further performance. Providing feedback to students refers to corrections, suggestions, or cues that are tailored to the individual's current performance and that encourage revision and refinement. Many learning studies have shown that students' learning improves and their understanding deepens when they are given timely and targeted feedback. However, feedback is not always effective.

In a meta-analysis of 131 studies, Kluger and DeNisi (1998) found that, on average, feedback interventions have only a moderate effect ($d = 0.4$) compared to providing no feedback. They also found that fully one third of the studies exhibited significant negative effects of feedback compared to no feedback at all. The negative effects of feedback were mostly associated with feedback that directed the learner's attention to the self rather than to the task or feedback that provided no specific information for improvement.

The activities in OLI courses provide feedback indicating where students are relative to the stated learning goal and what they need to do to improve. Such feedback does not simply tell the students that they are right or wrong, but rather gives clear information about how their performance differs from the target goal and what adjustments are needed to support them in reaching that goal. The system provides feedback on strengths and weaknesses, highlighting which aspects of their knowledge should be maintained and built upon and which aspects should be changed. The feedback given on specific actions is carefully designed to address common misconceptions and the incomplete or misapplied correct knowledge that such actions reflect. When done correctly, this can be very powerful. One student who received such feedback while working through an OLI activity was overheard saying, "How did the computer know what I was thinking?"

LOOKING AHEAD

Over the past 2 years, the focus and work on MOOCs have accelerated progress in knowledge about how to scale the delivery of some forms of instruction and how to collect and mine massive amounts of data. The OLI project and other learning technology projects have made progress in how to leverage learning research to inform the design of educational technologies to serve a diversity of students; how to structure the collection and analysis of data to improve instruction and refine learning theory; and how to engage faculty in transforming teaching and learning. The next phase of research and development in the use of technology in higher education can build on what has been learned from all of these approaches.

Ongoing research and adaptive management in designing learning environments is critical because the higher education context is in flux. The subject knowledge that students are expected to master is growing, as are the number and complexity of skills that students are expected to develop, the number of students who are expected to achieve a college degree, and the diversity in the student population. Happily, the scientific understanding of how people learn is also growing, and the technology is changing rapidly, along with the way people are using it. Information technology can offer ways of creating, over time, a complex stream of data about how students think and reason; this, in turn, can support adaptive decision-making.

Designing effective learning environments and data systems is not a small or inexpensive undertaking. It will require the cooperation of many institutions and faculty. The role of colleges and universities is to lead the process of improving higher education through sustained application of the science of learning to the design, broad use, evaluation, and ongoing improvement of learning environments. In leading this effort, higher education has the distinct advantage of having the faculty who possess the subject matter and research expertise, and the passion not only for their own fields of study but also for their students' learning. So while there is no quick panacea for the challenges confronting higher education, there is an envisioned process and a goal. The transformation of the nation's higher education system will be a multifaceted, multi-institutional, multiyear research and development process.

Why New Modes Are Not New Bottles for Old Wine

Ray Schroeder and Vickie Cook

CONTEXT OF THE NEW MODES OF EDUCATION

How many times have we heard that this or that new advancement will revolutionize higher education? Yet nothing of substance seems to change.

In 1800, James Pillans, headmaster of the Old High School of Edinburgh, Scotland, connected a number of smaller slates to create the first documented classroom blackboard (Buzbee, 2014). That may have been the last significant change for the next 200 years. By 1990, the classroom was little different than Pillans's in 1800. Sure, the blackboards at the front of the classroom had turned white, and dry erase pens had replaced chalk. Electronic tablets had replaced slate tablets for lecture note taking. But the lectern remained the central fixture at the front of the classroom. Classes still started at fixed times—often with the ringing of a bell. Students filed into the classroom on cue and were expected to listen intently and scribe the salient details of the lecture. Faculty members pontificated for an hour, or two, or three at a time. Education was teacher centered; there was little or no emphasis on differing student needs and goals. In many ways, this "factory" approach prepared youth for a lifetime of regimented work on the assembly line and the associated tight hierarchical framework of the industrial society.

For the 19th and most of the 20th century, these educational approaches seemed to serve societal needs well; students graduated, were employed, and pursued careers to retirement. Use of technology to meet the needs of emerging self-determined learners both in and out of the classroom continues to have a sustainable impact on the business of teaching and learning (Blaschke, 2012).

We saw education delivered through the medium of television; the "Sunrise Semester" ran for some 25 years beginning in 1957, but the format was not far different from the on-campus equivalent (Archives NYU). The classes began and ended at the same time; the communication still was mostly one-way. Instructional television classes were delivered at a distance via microwave networks to remote (satellite) locations across states. Yet the essential characteristics were the same. While a precious few programs emphasized service learning, internships, workshops, seminars, and no textbooks, the vast majority of classes were faculty centric; sessions were defined by rigidly set start and stop times; students were still treated just the same—little or no differentiation was afforded. *Education remained old wine in new bottles.*

Throughout the past decade, we have begun to see growing evidence of a student-centered model. Technology-enhanced learning is assisting the faculty who want to move students to the center of the learning (Schroeder, 2015).

Technology-enhanced learning is belatedly catching up with other advances. In the latter half of the 20th century, technological advances emerged that broadly shook the economy and society. In the late 1960s, the Department of Defense created DARPANET, linking select research universities, corporations, and federal research departments in a peer network to collaborate on the development of advanced computer-based structures and systems. This system evolved into the Internet. Meanwhile, the advent of the personal computer in the 1970s began to crack the paper culture that had prevailed since the advent of the printing press. The World Wide

Web built upon these advancements, making easy graphical access to the expanding Internet in the early 1990s and launching an Information Age that radically changed the needs of economies and societies worldwide.

The emergence of robotics increasingly replaced humans on the line by more accurately, consistently, and economically performing tasks than those who had filled those jobs in the past. Workforce needs changed. No longer was the pivotal worker in developed countries laboring on an assembly line. Corporations needed workers who could cope in a far less regimented structure, handling the data and constantly changing product lines and services. The Information Age swept across even farms and the rural culture. Enhanced computerized machinery and methods vastly improved productivity and became standard in agriculture. And with those changes came the need for farmers to have access to learning on a continuing basis to master the expanding and advancing technologies that were driving efficiency and competitiveness in the agro-economy.

These broad societal changes, driven by the enormous force of economies and efficiencies dictated by competition and emerging markets, in turn placed new demands on education. No longer were lifelong assembly line workers needed. The need largely evaporated for shift supervisors and specialized operational managers whose jobs would not change for decades at a time. Factories were no longer slow-changing operations employing thousands of workers performing repetitive tasks year after year. No longer did society need education to inculcate students with the regimentation of the factory-driven industrial economy. The educational approaches of the prior centuries had become outdated. Society no longer needed graduates schooled in the strict structures and repetition of the factory culture. Some radical changes needed to take place to meet the radically new demands of a postindustrial economy (Christensen, 2013; Hecht, 2013; Wiese & Christensen, 2014).

The advent of the Information Age meant that society needed creators, collaborators, and communicators who were facile and could think outside the box, instead of thousands of look-alike, think-alike employees whose goal was stability. Corporations needed workers who could adapt on a dime: learn new technologies, methods, and approaches—on the fly, without delay, without leaving the work-place. Continuing education was needed if employees were to advance to keep up with the changes in the corporation and the world at large.

The disconnect between education and the needs of society became obvious by the turn of the 21st century. Michelle Weise, senior research fellow in higher education at the Clayton Christensen Institute for Disruptive Innovation, put it well: "Something is clearly wrong when only 11% of business leaders—compared to 96% of chief academic officers—believe that graduates have the requisite skills for the workforce" (2014). And besides those graduates, there are the tens of millions of students who chose, or were forced, to drop out of higher education.

> [Thirty-one] million students have left college with-out earning a degree in the last 20 years, according to the National Student Clearinghouse Research Center, leaving a huge amount of almost-students degree bereft. Welcome to the term "potential completers": a specific set of students characterized by a set of personal issues (financial struggles, simple boredom, family concern, lack of time) that forces them to quit a traditional degree pathway, though ideally they'd like to continue with their education. (Bethke, 2014)

Yet the very technologies and economic pressures that put demands on economies and societies to demand more from education were also affording changes in education itself. Plummeting prices for computers and networks made these technologies accessible to education at all levels and at all locations. The vice chancellor of the Open University and founder of FutureLearn, the UK's leading MOOC provider, Martin Bean, feels that the Internet opened Pandora's box, as the Information Age revolution has begun to take hold in education:

> Disruptive innovation is forcing so many of us to reconsider the very foundations of our learning and teachings.... There isn't a higher education institution in the world that shouldn't be thinking about the role of technology and innovation.... This is something that's going to be a massive shift. (Murray, 2014)

HOW THE NEW MODES ARE INHERENTLY DIFFERENT

The new modes of teaching and learning are motivated and driven by something much larger than the preferences and conveniences of the higher education industry. They are transformative as well as transformed modes; they are not just new, but make learning happen in new and different ways. By their very nature, they will continue to evolve to meet the needs of society and the students.

No longer are these modes of education teacher centered. They are, instead, student centered, which is to say that both the attention and activity are centered on the student. These new modes are no longer designed for the convenience of the institution or the instructor. The focus is no longer on the lectern at the front of the room. The new approaches focus on the needs of the student. Teaching is differentiated for the different needs of the students rather than using a one-lecture-fits-all approach. This emphasis, on the student rather than on the teacher, is a radical departure from the classes of the past, pays off in ensuring that students are not left behind, that there can be differences in pacing and presentation. Students are constantly assessed to be sure that they understand the materials. Gone are the days in which there was one midterm and one final exam in a class. Now, more often, there are weekly assessments to identify what is clearly understood and what is not clear to each student. Immediate remediation is available in multiple modes ranging from text to case studies to video vignettes to ensure that the student's needs are addressed in the most effective mode for that individual student. In the new model, an array of support services, including tutors, peer tutors, advisers, mentors, and the faculty members, comprise an intervention team to ensure student learning. Supported by high-quality tutorial modules, the goal is to ensure mastery by every student. That is far from the all-too-common notion held previously that a rigorous quality course would produce a percentage of Ds and failures (and failures to complete) to match the percentage of As and Bs.

The new modes of education are different at their very core. They have emerged from the rapid growth of online and blended learning. They respond to the 21st-century students' facility with the tools of mobile communication. They respond to the demands of employers and the needs of students to address competencies rather than vaguely stated principles. The new modes leverage the data collection capability of learning management systems in blended and online programs to assess students' progress. Increasingly, these modes leverage more than merely the web; they build upon the growing infrastructure of the "Internet of Everything," employing intelligent sensors that react to personalize the experience of the learner (*How will the Internet of Everything change education by 2018?*). They apply both data and linkages to instantly support learning needs without requiring the student to access the support, much in the way mobile communication provides automatic updates and notifications.

MOBILE LEARNING

The students of the 21st century are mobile. They are on the move as they balance jobs and families, intellectual advancement and recreation. No longer are the majority of students living and learning full time on campus. They are working and learning while on the move.

Learning for nurses takes place in 10- to 15-minute breaks while on the hospital floor. Using a tablet or smartphone, a nurse may start a lecture module in the middle of the night shift in the corner of the nurses' station, resuming it on public transportation during the commute home. The nurse is looking up material while walking from the floor to the hospital staff cafeteria, composing reports using speech recognition dictation just as the nurse does in entering notes into the chart at the patient's bedside. Exchanges with the instructor and fellow students occur through the discussion board, VoiceThread, Google Hangouts, and chats that are hosted online. The learning process is woven into the fabric of the busy days and nights of the nurse's life. Learning is literally on the move with the nurse, as close as the smartphone, tablet, or wearable device.

This new mode of mobile learning is far different from the old mode of students going to the classroom as the site of learning, quietly sitting and waiting for the teacher to initiate the class session, and then sitting in the dormitory or library reading the textbook as the primary source of learning material. The new mode is much more flexible and mobile, more active and engaging. It becomes an integral part of the life of the student rather than a compartmentalized divergence from the other activities that make up the student's life.

COMPETENCY-BASED LEARNING

The new modes of learning are designed to develop acquired competencies (and allow the student to demonstrate them). Learning outcomes defined in terms of competencies are what map the learning process. Older modes of education would define courses in terms of *subjects* rather than outcomes. To be fair, there may have been objectives along the way in those courses. But far too often, the focus was not clear to either the instructor or the students. More often than not, the course was the sum of the textbook chapters, and the objective, in a word, was coverage. Learning in a course was an ill-defined 15-week program of exposure to content.

The new modes of education define far more clearly the outcomes of classes in terms of competencies that will be demonstrated by the student. These can be demonstrated within the context of a class or outside that context as competencies gained through work or other experience. The focus of the new modes is to climb the pyramid of Bloom's taxonomy from the basics of remembering and understanding to learning's higher order levels of evaluating and creating.

In older modes of education, the student would peruse the syllabus as a loose amalgam of reading assignments, tests, and perhaps a final paper, which would be submitted at the end of the class, too late for formative assessment to occur. Often, the syllabus would not include any reference to learning outcomes, objectives, or competencies. The student would progress sequentially through the textbook, taking quizzes on memorized facts from each chapter. The course would be aimed at the lower orders of Bloom's taxonomy: remembering and understanding. In too many classes, the student experience would not rise above those lower orders, excepting a single venture into the next order of applying what was learned in the final paper. The goal of the course was to remember and understand the subject.

Instructional design as part of the new modes of education has evolved to begin not with the selection of a textbook but rather with defining the learning objectives and the competencies that the students are to achieve by the end of the course. In other words, course design begins with outcomes and determines the ways to build the desired competencies. New approaches include frequent assessments to ensure that students are making good progress each step along the way. Learning employs scaffolding, building upon knowledge and skills that have come before. Formative evaluations are a critical part of the process, assessing students' progress through their learning experiences as they occur.

In the older modes of education, an engineering student would progress through classes by learning facts and formulas. Textbooks would define the learning, week by week, month by month. Lectures would restate the facts and formulas in the textbook. Tests would be administered to ensure that the facts and formulas were committed to memory. A final exam would test the memorization of the student, the ability to retain the cumulative store of facts, phrases, and formulas for the semester.

In newer modes of education, engineering students (for example) may not attend live, unrecorded lectures at all. The necessary facts, formulas, and principles are available online to be studied outside of class and ready for retrieval by a mobile device on a moment's notice. One model, the flipped classroom, devotes class time to working together with other students on hands-on projects. The faculty member is present to work with the groups of students as they complete engineering projects that apply the principles learned online. Together, the groups of students apply, analyze, and evaluate their work in projects and the work of other groups. They thereby utilize higher order learning activities, as defined by Bloom's taxonomy, including analyzing, evaluating, and creating. Toward the end of the term, the engineering students are tasked with creating a final product using the principles, facts, and formulas they learned online, coupled with the experience gained from applying, analyzing, and evaluating prior projects. With the new modes of education, students are far from relying on the textbook, often utilizing professional resources and open data sets from online sources instead. The final projects are not feats of memory like final exams but demonstrations of the competencies built into the design of the course. They are also tangible evidence of competencies sought by employers, curated in the student's e-portfolio.

MODULARITY

The Massachusetts Institute of Technology (MIT), after a significant self-study, led the way to open educational resources more than a dozen years ago when it announced that, on the principle that learning resources should be freely available, the university would put online the resources from as many of its classes as possible. This leadership resulted in a tidal wave of texts, lectures, references, and educational tools being shared worldwide (Carr, 2013). While quite innovative at the time, the movement is now 14 years old and part of the old wine (lectures, reading lists, etc.). Still, the movement continues today. More recently, in the summer of 2014, MIT completed another self-study and announced that it would pursue an initiative to break classes into modules. Calling this a "historic opportunity to reinvent the residential campus model and perhaps redefine education altogether," President L. Rafael Reif announced the MIT Initiative for Educational Innovation. A key feature of the initiative is the offering of online, on-demand modules for students seeking access to discrete areas of knowledge. The report says that the very notion of a class may be outdated:

This in many ways mirrors the preferences of students on campus. The unbundling of classes also reflects a larger trend in society—a number of other media offerings have become available in modules, whether it is a song from an album, an article from a newspaper, or a chapter from a textbook. (Bradt, 2014)

This move toward modules builds upon competency-based approaches by further defining learning outcomes into discrete modules with specific learning goals. The ability to stack learning modules together allows students to create customizable, functional learning credentials. For example,

a student in a[n] MBA program and another studying nursing might have similar learning objectives but draw upon different content and materials to achieve those learning objectives. This flexible architecture, which technology enhances, enables online competency-based providers to create and scale a multitude of stackable credentials or programs for a wide variety of industries. (Weise & Christensen, 2014)

The modular approach represents an important change, shifting at least some determination of curriculum design from the academic department to the student. It allows students to stack together custom credentials to meet the needs of emerging careers and employers. In stacking modules, students can, in a sense, develop their own curriculum. Those selections can also be made on the advice of employers. In either case, the university curriculum committee does not drive the decisions as in the past. The curriculum itself is constructed by the student from the smaller modules developed by faculty. This moves the curriculum closer to the needs of the student and the employer, where it is most useful.

DATA-DRIVEN LEARNING

Learning management systems offer the first opportunity in the history of education to collect meaningful quantitative data on the learning process in every class for each student. These data enable *descriptive analytics* to delineate in detail the characteristics of students and their learning behaviors. The descriptive data include prior education, demographic data, and details that may positively or negatively affect learning for the student. Data dashboards now monitor activities and issue warnings as well as success signals based on even subtle performance changes. As the student progresses through the curriculum, additional data are collected that include learning style preferences and associated characteristics. These enable *predictive analytics* to predict successes and failures. And where the data predict failures, they enable *prescriptive analytics* to recommend interventions that have proven to be successful for students with similar characteristics in such circumstances. These data-driven approaches are far different from the educational modes of the past, where students were left to their own devices to thrive or fail without detection or intervention.

A student in a past course in Greek history, for example, would be left alone to do the reading assigned for the class. Several weeks into the class, the instructor would not know how much time the student had spent on reading or whether the student was successfully learning the content. During class sessions, the instructor might ask probing questions but only hear from the same handful of students who reliably raised their hands out of the class's three dozen students. Essays could be required for each reading, but with nearly a dozen readings and three dozen students, the instructor needed to read hundreds of essays to get a full sense of the class's engagement with the material, taking away valuable time from possibly interacting with students. Quizzes could also be assigned in class to ensure that the students had memorized the essential facts and characters of each reading. The emphasis is, once again, on the lower order learning of remembering and understanding the texts.

In the new modes of education, students are monitored as they complete reading assignments. Data are collected as they are quizzed several times a week to see if they are not just keeping up with the reading but also picking up on the nuances of the writing. The data collected reflect how long the students linger over questions, which wrong answers they choose, and how much time they spend on reading what's assigned online. In other words, the data reflect how learning occurs, with what frequency, at what pace, through what format. Wrong answers on quizzes automatically trigger brief tutorials individualized based on student learning preferences to help the student understand what may have been missed. These *adaptive* approaches to the delivery of quizzes and tutorials create an inventory of the study preferences of the students. What is more important, these approaches much more thoroughly assess the learning of students who may not raise their hands as often or as quickly as others in class. Essays are still assigned and initially graded by the instructor, but using expert system technologies, the grading patterns of the instructor are "learned" by software that increasingly takes over grading the essays semester by semester (Menon, 2013). Currently, this type of "robo-grading" may require a sample of up to 1,000 or more faculty-graded essays to establish a clearly consistent evaluation of student work, and its effectiveness remains under critique (Perelman, 2013).

Class time, whether in person or via synchronous online sessions, is spent in small groups analyzing and evaluating the authors' writing, themes, and meanings. Data dashboards monitor student participation in group discussions and help the instructor better determine the engagement of each student. In a case where engagement seems low, the instructor can spend more time interacting with that student and finding out what the problem seems to be. Finally, each student develops a project that draws upon the learning in the group sessions.

THE SYNERGY OF THE NEW MODES OF EDUCATION: SELF-ACTUALIZING LEARNING

An increasing synergy is becoming evident in the collective use of student-centered, competency-based, technology-enhanced, mobile-enabled, data-directed education. This combination of characteristics is leading to some greater effects that add up to more than simply the sum of their parts. It seems to be a natural outcome of the combination of these new modes, so often user centered, that education is becoming more self-actualizing, allowing students to take control of and responsibility for their learning. This approach to learning is the foundation of the theory of heutagogical learning (Blaschke, 2012). New learning modes are spontaneously arising at the nexus of needs and opportunities. Increasingly, student learning is credentialed through badges and alternative certifications.

In responding to the larger trends of the economy and to industry needs, and in drawing upon the advances in technologies and techniques, the new modes have generated personal learning networks (PLNs). Capitalizing on social networking, open educational resources, and mobile technologies, personal learning that leads to recognized competencies is beginning to take place outside formal education structures. Self-paced and self-directed learning can allow for the identification of competencies that are in demand or about to become in demand. Through the new modes of learning, students will be enabled to lead the way in designing new virtual degrees and certificates. With the prospect of students directing the forces at play in higher education, institutions must create new opportunities for students to have input into the modes they are interested in utilizing. They should also have opportunities to be self-directed in their approaches to learning, ideally sustaining a desire to learn throughout their lives as they need additional information, applicability, and ways to manage the information they are interested in exploring (Craig, 2014). The amalgamation of these approaches has prompted discussion of reinventing college.

Stanford's Design School has acknowledged these changes and is examining radical ideas for reinventing college in light of these changes. Sarah Stein Greenberg, executive director of the school, suggests that today's education system is resulting in "a generation of students who are incredibly highly structured, but they're going to be entering an increasingly ambiguous world." Instead, Greenberg says, "We need to be training our students not to just expect that they will be society's leaders, but also to be our most creative, daring, and resilient problem solvers" (Vanhemert, 2014).

The new modes of education may enable future students to do just that. Institutions outside of the United States are also rethinking the concepts related to the structure and organization of higher education policies and systems. Nova Scotia's Minister of Labor and Advanced Education recently described the higher education system as "unsustainable" (Davis & Whalen, 2014). The 2015 New Media Consortium (NMC) Horizon Report identified the need for visionary and innovative leaders to encourage and sustain growth within higher education: "In order to breed innovation and adapt to economic needs, higher education institutions must be structured in ways that allow for flexibility, and spur creativity and entrepreneurial thinking" (Johnson, Becker, Estrada, & Freeman, 2015).

CONCLUSION

The new modes of education are dramatically and demonstrably different from the modes we have experienced in the past. Education in the 21st century puts the student rather than the instructor at the center of the process. Education has become outward looking as well, serving industries and employers as it serves students. The changes we are seeing are pushed in part by a towering student debt of more than $1 trillion and pulled by employers and industries desperately seeking new kinds of employees—employees who are self-actualized, motivated, and responsive to change. The new modes are both push and pull, sustained by the dynamic energy built between the student and the employer (Weise, 2014).

Still more changes will evolve quickly, perhaps even by the time this publication is released. Yet this list of terms provides educators and decision-makers with some touchstones to catalyze a rethinking of their perceptions about approaches to learning in higher education:

- moving from pedagogy to andragogy to heutagogy;
- authentic assessment;
- data gathering and analysis to
  - describe,
  - prescribe,
  - predict, and
  - assess;
- differentiated learning;
- personalized learning;
- adaptive learning;
- moving from online learning to on-demand learning;
- competency transcripting;
- modularization; and

- alternative degrees and credentials, including
  - nanodegrees and
  - stackable credentials.

Encouraging higher order learning, the new modes capitalize on the technologies that afford mobility and flexibility to students and professors, but their affordances may matter still more to those who will employ the students as graduates. The value factors for employers have moved up the pyramid of Bloom's taxonomy. It is now far less about what you know or remember than it is about how you can apply, analyze, evaluate, and create. Data are easily uncovered in this Google Age; it is what employees can creatively do with information that is of value in the 21st-century economy.

A key value in the transition from education to employment that has been flawed in the older modes of education is the clear articulation of outcomes and competencies of learning. A college transcript currently does little to communicate what the student has learned. An A or B in a course titled Rhetoric speaks very little to what was learned and what the student can do. The move to modularization and competency-based learning provides more clarity to what a transcript can convey. Adding badges that certify competencies is a welcome addition to all and an improvement that employers will not surrender.

The new modes of education will continue to evolve and respond to the needs of both students and employers. It seems likely that students will be drawn to those universities that offer them new-found freedom to participate in designing their curriculum; enhanced technologically delivered support; self-paced, adaptive learning; and more seamless transition to employment. Those colleges and universities that embrace the changes are more likely to survive and may well thrive.

So, yes, change is needed. It does not make a difference whether those faculty and administrators in higher education are ready or not. It does not matter whether they think it is too fast or not. Frankly, it does not matter whether they agree to change or not. Students and employers are now leading the charge. By failing to respond in time to the external changes of the economy and society as well as technology, higher education has abdicated the role of leading change. It can regain its leadership only by guiding change to maximum effect with more focus and research on innovations, more faculty development, and more thoughtful adoption of new modes.

Key Conclusions | What the Changing Modes of Learning Are and Mean

Plus ça change.... Thinking about change runs in such a well-worn groove that we don't need the rest of the famous French expression to know the foregone conclusion. But thinking that the more things change the more they stay the same may make us miss the change that really changes things. The truth is that we know much more about learning than we used to. And the modes of learning we have now can inform the learning process as it is happening. Combining this new analytic depth with vastly expanded scale and scope promises to be truly transformative.

CANDACE THILLE'S KEY CONCLUSIONS:

- While research in learning was not lacking, instructional practice lagged significantly behind—at a remove in time, place, and academic register. But new modes of learning put research and instruction in contact with each other in a recursive cycle of input and feedback.
- This research and development cycle allows the learning process to be improved significantly, with that improvement demonstrated by better learning outcomes, often in shorter time frames and other important departures from established practice.
- The growing knowledge of the learning process is so important because the body of knowledge students must learn, together with the requisite skills, is also growing. Monitored, adaptive instruction is critical to helping higher

education keep pace with all that today's (and tomorrow's) students must learn.

RAY SCHROEDER AND VICKIE COOK'S KEY CONCLUSIONS:

- Until recently, changes in education, even when using technology, really changed nothing essential because they remained faculty centric. The new modes are student centered as well as technology mediated.
- The difference the new modes manifest is a response to changes in society, with a greater emphasis on access and connection, continuous feedback and improvement, and greater adaptability and modularization.
- Greater clarity about competencies and the assessments for these allows the new modes to coalesce around synergies of self-actualized learning and targeted credentialing; students and employers can know that they are getting what they need, and it behooves higher education to deliver.

The authors in this section are very aware of the investment the greater change they are calling for will take and the resistance it will have to overcome. The next section explains how such change can and should take place, both at the level of the institution and across the complex and stratified system of higher education.

SECTION 4:

Managing Change

The challenge of change is that it is always plural—always, by definition, varied and variable in impact and effect. We live in a welter of changes. Some seem simply to happen, often coming as surprises or incursions; others are lobbied for and sought after. Some seem superficial, mere trends of the moment, vicissitudes that change nothing in essence, like changes in fashion. Others seem deeply disruptive, changing the landscape or the rules of the game. Managing change means first of all distinguishing kinds of change and their consequences, then guiding what can be guided and steeling for what must be met with. Any change that matters demands a response; managing to respond, and respond meaningfully, is really what managing change is all about.

Such wisdom for our changeful time is precisely what the authors in this section offer. In "Strategic Decision-Making in an Emergent World," James Hilton and James DeVaney begin by presenting the perspectives of younger versions of themselves, a professor and a student navigating a world changed by technology. Their users' perspective is critical: Thinking through it, whether the impact is to instructional media or downloadable music, lets them see the changes that matter and the lessons to be learned, ultimately for one of the great flagship campuses among our public universities. In "A Delicate Balance: Promoting University Change in the 21st Century," Jonathan R. Cole begins with resistance to change at one of the nation's great private universities. But he also sees and shows research universities as key drivers of progress, introducing the great innovations of the past century. The research with which to meet and even shape the future was long undergirded by a compact of support now eroding. Moving forward requires action on a number of levels, from a rethinking of federal support to a commitment to internal institutional reform.

Strategic Decision-Making in an Emergent World

James Hilton and James DeVaney

Maybe fate brought us to this moment. In the late 1990s, we were both at the University of Michigan. James Hilton was toying with the idea of moving from being a full-time faculty member to being a faculty member and an administrator. James DeVaney was living the life of a college student, wide open to what would come. Though we lived in largely separate worlds, we both found ourselves spending an enormous amount of time wrestling with a technology that, on the surface at least, did not look like it had much of anything to do with higher education. Indeed, it was a technology that many dismissed as little more than a parlor trick.

DR. DRE, METALLICA, AND COUZENS HALL

James Hilton's brush with the technology came in the context of teaching introductory psychology. He was trying to introduce technology and rich media into a course that enrolled more than 1,000 students. At every turn, however, he was confronted with a conflict between what technology enabled and what copyright law and university policy allowed. What materials could be shown in class versus put on the web? Did anyone have the right to take notes in class and sell them to students? Who owned the new digital tools that were being developed in the context of teaching?

What were the relationships between the works that faculty did as scholars versus teachers versus committee members?

In grappling with these questions, Hilton did what many do. He complained—and was rewarded with a committee assignment. He was asked to chair a committee that would look at those issues, which led to a report, which led to an administrative assignment and a fairly rapid descent into the world of bureaucracy.

Somewhere in the midst of that sojourn, he heard a discussion between two audiophiles on NPR about this new audio format called MP3s and whether MP3s would replace the format found on CDs. After discussing the inferior sound quality of the new format, both confidently rejected the notion that it was anything more than a technical curiosity. And in a moment reminiscent of the Far Side cartoon in which all but one member of a group of self-assured dinosaurs make fun of the awkward-looking furry mammal just as the snow begins to fall, one of the audiophiles closed out the interview by saying something to the effect of *You know, the sound quality really is quite awful, but the file size is remarkably small. You could email a song in this format to someone if you wanted to.* It was an observation that presaged decades of turmoil in the music industry.

Meanwhile, on the other side of campus and six floors above Palmer Field, James DeVaney huddled in a cozy dorm room around a second-hand microwave, loft furniture, and a space-eating CD collection with the coed residents of Couzens Hall. It was the fall of 1997, and the musical gods had answered the price-elastic prayers of an impatient band of college freshmen whose existing music collections were likely their most valuable assets. Tethered to the wall by a bright yellow Ethernet cord, computer monitors emitted a glow that served as a spotlight into a world of on-demand, un-bundled, sharable entertainment. A single click, and one's personal catalog changed.

Mesmerized by this new experience, DeVaney did what many would do. He didn't complain—and was rewarded with new recommendations, real-time sharing, and relationships. Who could notice the sound quality as the shared experience and collection were enhanced with each completed transfer? He joined a networked world, which led to new expectations, which led to a different set of choices and a fairly rapid ascent into the digital era.

Was the quality the same as that of the CD purchased down the street at the record store that now no longer exists? Not even close. But these listeners desired more than one kind of experience. It wasn't so much about the quality of the audio as it was about other things: the immediacy of the experience (any music was just a click away); the social nature of the experience ("sharing" brought the opportunity to influence and be influenced by the collections and preferences of peers); and a richer and more differentiated experience of music (the world was no longer dictated by choices producers made, as *albums* gave way to *playlists* and *listening* gave way to *ripping, mixing, and burning*). The consumer became producer, critic, influencer, and curator.

The song wars had begun. In September 2000, lawyers for Dr. Dre and Metallica sent letters to prominent universities, including the University of Michigan, asking us to block Napster from our networks and making vaguely threatening noises about litigation (Borland, 2000). An industry that had survived numerous technology shifts with its basic business model intact (e.g., wax to vinyl to tape to CD) now found itself grappling with technologies that it could not control (i.e., "perfect" copies, "free" distribution networks, and peer-to-peer interactions). It hesitated. It reacted. It resorted to suing the very people it wanted to be its customers. And while it did that, the computer industry, primarily in the guise of Apple, found ways to rebundle music, meet and create customer demand, and extract revenue. In 1999, total U.S. sales of recorded music amounted to $14.6 billion; in 2008, that number had dropped to $6.3 billion (Goldman, 2010). In the same period, Apple's market cap went from $9 billion to $84 billion (Wikinvest, 2015). Today, Apple's market cap is at $640 billion. The demand for music never waned. The players and the models of delivery, revenue, and control, however, changed dramatically.

HIGHER EDUCATION CIRCA 2015

Spinning from the record to the quadrangle, what lessons should we take from the music industry's recent history? Higher education today finds itself confronted by a cacophony of instruments vying for time from anyone who will listen: platforms and tools, massive open online courses (MOOCs) and self-paced open courses (SPOCs), analytics and content repositories. It is a noisy time to think about the future of higher education. To quote the great Sidney Deane from the movie *White Men Can't Jump*: "Look man, you can listen to Jimi but you can't hear him. There's a difference, man. Just because you're listening to him doesn't mean you're hearing him." Higher education is clearly listening to the changing world around us. A quick glance at the headlines in any given week is likely to find stories about tuition spirals, student debt, the promise/threat of on-line education, the relative decline in education levels in the United States, and a host of other topics that all point to an intense interest in higher education at this moment in time. It's incredibly noisy out there. So how do we filter out the noise to hear the music? How do we separate the signal from the noise in times of disruptive change?

The recording industry maintained a bundled product, experi-enced growth and perceived invincibility for a considerable time, survived many technology revolutions, and created new rules (e.g., the Digital Millennium Copyright Act) to enforce their business model. While we believe that the parallels between the unbundling of music and the current disruptions in higher education are valid, our focus here is not on these similarities. Instead, it is on moving from passively *listening* to the changing world around us to actively *hearing* it. It is about four lessons that we can adopt to make better strategic decisions in a world where technology changes quickly and often in disruptive ways. We'll explore the lessons first and then explore an approach to making strategic decisions by navigating an emergent world.

LESSON 1: CHANGE IS MESSY AND EMERGENT

One challenge in dealing with a rapidly changing environment is that our everyday conceptions of change don't serve us well. We tend to think of change as orderly and planned. Like rows of corn planted neatly in a field or arrow-straight irrigation ditches rolling through the arid West, traditional models of change assume that change is planned, intentional, orderly, and coherent. The reality of change is that it tends to show up messy. The world is more the result of complex adaptive systems than it is of orderly, planned progression. Complex adaptive systems have four characteristics: multiple agents act in parallel; agents' actions influence one another; responses (behavioral routines) are recruited and evaluated on the fly; and agents adapt and evolve over time (Holland, 2006). As a result, change in a complex adaptive system is less like a production assembly line than it is like the shifting river channels in the Amazon.

As an example of emergent change via complex adaptive systems, consider the University of Michigan. Founded in 1817 as one of the nation's first public universities, it was designed to provide class-room instruction to its students. It did and does that, of course, but the deeper point is how it has emerged from that relatively simple vision. At its inception, no one would have predicted 19 schools and colleges, an academic medical center that generates half the revenue of the university, the rise of the research university, more than 1,000 student organizations, or the role of the Big House and football in the life of the campus. Those emerged in response to forces that were largely outside the university's plan. Instead, they resulted from the actions of many, operating in parallel, influencing one another, and adapting and reacting.

LESSON 2: IN THE FACE OF DISRUPTIVE CHANGE, FOCUS ON UNDERSTANDING FUNDAMENTAL CONDITIONS

Acknowledging that people who preach disruption typically overestimate the short-term impact, they also tend to underestimate the long-term impact. On the one hand, we were supposed to be commuting by jetpack and hoverboards in 2015. On the other, the printing press inked the Reformation, the rise of democracy, and the Age of Enlightenment (Naughton, 2012). In a world filled with hype and talk of disruptive change, how do we distinguish between passing trends and fundamental conditions? How do we identify the underlying conditions that call most for attention?

We confess, we're not sure. We haven't been able to identify a formula or procedure that automatically separates the wheat from the chaff when it comes to substantive versus superficial forces. But what we do think is possible is to look at the landscape in which higher education finds itself and look for the recurring themes, trends, and facts that you ignore at your peril.

Consistent with the view that *fundamental conditions* are relatively small in number, we nominate three that seem inextricably linked to the digital education era and that every institution should be planning around:

SHIFTING DEMOGRAPHICS AND PUBLIC ATTENTION

Ask any candidate for a high-level administrative job at a public university what they would seek to change if given the job, and you will likely get an earful about the need for the state to increase its support of higher education. We agree. But here's the thing: We think it is highly unlikely to happen. The demographic bubble that supported disproportionate investment in education over the past century has moved on to health care and dying. It's not coming back. State governments find themselves confronted with challenges associated with aging populations and infrastructures that create immediate and irresistible demands on the states' budgets.

But the shift is more fundamental than state budgets. The attention of the public has moved on. Higher education is increasingly seen as a burden more than an opportunity. Twenty years ago, a debate about the economic value of a college degree was inconceivable. Today, questioning the value of a college degree is in danger of becoming the default in the public conversation about the value of higher education. Going forward, the focus will remain relentlessly on reducing costs and proving direct economic value. The demographic answer is predetermined: Higher education has to be cheaper, faster, and better—a trifecta that many might argue is unobtainable.

THE UNRAVELING OF THE CREDIT-HOUR ECONOMY

Most institutions operate on a credit-hour economy in which classes are priced similarly, regardless of the cost of delivering them, and bundled together into degrees. Even though the costs to the institution are significantly different, large introductory lecture classes cost students the same as small seminars. The system works as long as there are enough low-cost courses to subsidize the delivery of high-cost courses in a degree. But that economy is poised to unravel for two reasons. First, much of the curriculum (i.e., introductory lecture-based courses) is fairly standard and subject to commodity pricing. Straighterline.com offers all the accredited courses you can drink for $99 a month. As financial pressures and cost consciousness increase, what happens to the model as students start to substitute low-cost online alternatives for introductory courses and continue to take the advanced courses in residence? Degree-granting institutions might respond by requiring that all the classes be taken from their institution, but that move runs counter to political pressure to increase the transferability of credit hours and feels a little bit like the recording industry trying to adjust the rules to protect an incumbent model. At the extreme, every institution needs to be planning against a world in which an accredited degree will be essentially free. It won't be the degree of that institution, but it will be an accredited degree.

Second, the whole notion of what constitutes a *course* or a *degree* is in flux. Coursera offers a rapidly growing catalog of MOOCs. Some of those MOOCs last as long as 14 weeks and resemble their residential counterparts quite closely. Others are as short as 4 weeks and look more like an episode of public television than a classroom. While you cannot yet get traditional course credit for the majority of Coursera courses, you can get a certificate for the courses you complete successfully. And before scoffing at the notion that certificates have no real value, it's worth noting that certificates are the second most frequently awarded credential from degree-granting institutions (González, 2012). Colleges and universities now award more certificates than they do associate, master's, or PhD degrees.

More generally, our conceptions of what a course is, what credit is, and what a degree is are in rapid transition, and higher education is not totally in control of the conversation.

INFORMATION UBIQUITY IN A NETWORKED ENVIRONMENT

Much like the recording industry, where the shift from vinyl to tape had little impact on the music business, most technologies that burble through the academy have minimal impact on the classroom. Television didn't change the classroom very much. We have had *distance education* via a variety of methods for decades now. So how should we view the current attention that digital education is getting? Are technologies like MOOCs, which allow for increasingly individualized content navigation delivered at Internet scale, going to revolutionize learning, as their proponents predict, or will they be just another technology fad, as their critics claim?

Perhaps not surprisingly, we are betting on lasting impact. What's different about today's technology is that it combines information ubiquity, which has been around pretty much since the invention of the book, with real-time interaction between students and instructors at scale. In other words, what's different is the combination of content abundance and communication networks that allow instantaneous interaction around that content. Today's online technology enables a level of interaction that sometimes exceeds the interaction in traditional face-to-face classes. Although many courses do not yet take advantage of that enablement, they will. To harken again to the comparison with the recording industry, it was the combination of perfect copies and network distribution that proved disruptive. We believe the combination of content and interaction is altering the learning landscape in important ways.

LESSON 3: DISCOVER A NORTH STAR

Despite our claims to the contrary, most institutions of higher education describe themselves similarly. Go on any tour of any campus with prospective students and this will become painfully evident. With rare exception, guides will talk about the unique experiences students will have at University X. They will emphasize the quality and quantity of interactions with the faculty. They will proselytize about the opportunities students have to conduct research as part of their education. They will highlight various combinations of service, global engagement, and experiential learning that are available to students. And they will talk from direct experience about the fruits of the cocurricular life. Regardless of whether the college is large or small, research intensive or mastery focused, rural or urban, the "pitch" is stunningly similar.

If you don't have the opportunity to go on college recruiting tours, take a look at the mission statements of your favorite cross section of secular schools. Odds are, they too will be stunningly similar. Indeed, we are pretty confident that if you print 20 of them off in plain text, put them in a paper bag, shake it up, and then draw the statements out and try to match them with their institution, you will be hard pressed to do better than random chance. Almost all of the mission statements emphasize the schools' commitments to scholarship, teaching, civic engagement, and personal attention. All aim to produce model citizens who are capable of critical thinking and ready to engage with the world.

In contrast to our public personae, within the academy we have a highly differentiated view of the landscape. We know which institutions are strong in which areas. We know that different institutions have different cultures. We know that institutions vary in their approaches and commitments to undergraduate and graduate education. We know that some institutions are deeply connected to their immediate surroundings and communities; some scarcely at all. But publicly we choose to emphasize our similarities rather than our differences (beyond the broad claim that we each do things better than anyone else).

In a growth economy, which higher education has enjoyed for most of its history, blurring differences between institutions is a fine strategy. If demand outstrips supply, if students are clamoring for admission, having a fairly undifferentiated public view of higher education works. But as we move to an increasingly constrained resource environment, and as viable alternatives to traditional models of education gain traction, the pressure on institutions to differentiate from each other will increase. As we move from a seller's market to a buyer's market, the pressure to articulate and defend an institution's unique value and performance will increase. Just as homebuyers become more selective in a housing glut, so will students become more selective as their options increase. And student choice is increasing at an exhilarating rate: a result of changing demographics, innovative approaches at traditional institutions, and new learning experiences enabled by new entrants to the field.

From our perspective, increased pressure to differentiate is not a bad thing. The educational experiences that students get at small liberal arts colleges are and should be different from the experiences they get at research-intensive institutions. Similarly, the experiences students have in residential programs will necessarily be different from the experiences they have in purely online programs. Indeed, the pressure to differentiate provides an opportunity for institutions to determine those things that they do best and that drive their institutions—an opportunity to find their institutional true north and use that to guide strategic decisions. And from the perspective of the students, having a coherent and differentiated view of the landscape would enable and empower students to make better educational choices. Everyone wins if the students and institutions wind up being better matched.

LESSON 4: DON'T MISTAKE BUYING TECHNOLOGY WITH INNOVATION

In 2003, Nicholas Carr launched a debate about the strategic value of information technology (IT) by claiming that as IT became ubiquitous, it lost strategic value (Carr, 2003). While the debate is vigorous (e.g., Brown & Hagel, 2003) and we don't agree entirely with Carr, there is an unhealthy tendency to assume that technology somehow automatically buys differentiation. Universities bought expensive enterprise resource planning systems (ERPs) in part because they promised access to information about business processes and resource use that could be tweaked to competitive advantage. The move ignored the fact that competitive advantage in the university ecosystem rarely derives from efficiency. It derives primarily from the reputations of the faculty, staff, and students.

Similarly, we have seen more than a decade focused on learning management systems (LMSs) as if the latest bells and whistles that accompany an LMS are likely to alter the competitive position of the school. They won't. ERPs and LMSs are infrastructure, not differentiators. Indeed, we believe it is time for the academy to move to a common shared infrastructure and focus more attention on how to use that shared infrastructure in ways that differentiate. Bottom line, going forward the focus should be on what institutions *do* with technology—how they use it to foster interaction, discovery, and mastery—and not which technology they have adopted. In other words, it is not a set of technology choices but our decision-making around what shared technology enables that has deep implications for the choices we make (Hilton, 2014).

STRATEGIC DECISION-MAKING IN AN ERA OF RAPID CHANGE AND DIFFERENTIATION

If change is more emergent than planned, strategic decision-making in a world of emergence is more akin to sailing and navigating open waters than it is to driving along a well-mapped highway. Project management and traditional multiyear planning increasingly fit less well in an emergent world. Strategy in an emergent world involves understanding the fundamental conditions that are shaping the environment and then using and reacting to those conditions in ways that bias things in the direction you want. Strategy is about recognizing a finite set of underlying conditions and incorporating them into the process of planning, acting, and adjusting. It assumes that the world is dynamic—that no plan survives contact with the world completely intact. It places greater emphasis on direction-setting and measuring progress than on creating detailed change-management plans. It requires institutions to be intentional about where they want to head, realistic about the conditions in which they find themselves, and vigilant in assessing progress and alignment.

Viewed this way, the four lessons above should not be mistaken for a road map. Instead, we see them as essential habits to guide decision-making. They provide a framing for taking and managing risks with technology in today's higher education landscape.

CASE STUDY: THE UNIVERSITY OF MICHIGAN

In an emergent digital era with significant resource constraints, how should a large research university like the University of Michigan prioritize and make strategic decisions? Disruptive change is challenging, in large part, because the very premise of disruptive change is that something in the environment changes that renders a set of long-held assumptions moot. Given the pace of change, fundamental conditions, and need for differentiation, where should institutions head next? Education leaders must be prepared to approach strategic decision-making as navigation. They and their institutions need to prepare to deliver education for this century and this economy with rapidly changing technology. In 2013, the University of Michigan created an office of Digital Education & Innovation (DEI) to provide a focal point for experimentation and planning around the disruptions and opportunities that digital technology enables. How have the four lessons above been applied to the launch?

LESSON 1: CHANGE IS MESSY AND EMERGENT— EXPERIMENT, LEARN, AND APPLY

If there is a single philosophy that permeates the University of Michigan, it is a deep and abiding commitment to diversity in all of its forms. That commitment led to a courtroom defense of the university's affirmative action policies premised on the notion that a diverse learning environment is, in fact, a better learning environment. Diverse environments provide multiple, often conflicting, perspectives that force more sophisticated analysis and understanding (Gurin, Nagda, & Lopez, 2004).

In the digital education space, that commitment to diversity shows up as a tendency to favor "a thousand flowers blooming" over large "all in" bets on direction/strategy. When given the opportunity to join edX or Coursera, for example, the university chose Coursera primarily because it provided a lower barrier to widespread experimentation. Coursera did not require a significant capital investment to join, and that allowed us to launch many courses on the Coursera platform. As of February 2015, we had created 24 MOOCs that had reached more than 2.5 million lifelong learners. We were also able to invest in other areas like learning analytics, flipped classrooms, and more gameful approaches to instructional design. Our approach to investment and experimentation has allowed us to remain learner centric and free to experiment with a range of tools and technologies in the service of innovative teaching and learning.

Similarly, Michigan, unlike many of our peers, has tended to avoid investing in global campuses. It's not that we fail to recognize the importance of globalization. Indeed, in recognition of its importance, an office of Global and Engaged Learning was created at approximately the same time as an office of Digital Education & Innovation (DEI). Instead, Michigan's approach to this space is also one of experimenting, learning, and scaling. The interests of our faculty are too diverse, and the expectation of evidence too high, to support large speculative investments.

In an emergent world, Michigan's approach is to identify potential innovations, test them, find pathways to scale, and institutionalize learning through the creation of prototypes, resources, and relationships. We experiment, learn, and winnow ahead of large investments that are pitched as "transformational."

In 2014, we formalized this approach by creating the Office of DEI to help the University of Michigan investigate new things and find pathways to scale. In an emergent world, DEI was created to make and guide strategic investments in curricular innovation, learning analytics, and digital infrastructure at scale. DEI is uniquely positioned to connect members of our community with one another and to prototypes, resources, and expertise across our academic innovation ecosystem.

DEI consists of four parts:

1 | The Digital Education & Innovation Lab (DEIL) serves as a collaborative learning space where faculty can experiment with digital tools and platforms, explore media production capabilities, discover new pedagogical techniques, and create new digital programs.

2 | The Learning, Education, & Design Lab (LED Lab) serves as a campus resource for collaboration and consultation on research projects that investigate the design and use of learning technologies in higher education.

3 | The Digital Innovation Greenhouse (DIG) cultivates and scales to maturity new digital education tools arising from Michigan's research community, establishing pathways to scale through collaboration across the University of Michigan's digital ecosystem.

4 | The DEI Venture Fund allows us make strategic investments in digital learning and pair those financial resources with expertise from the DEIL, LED Lab, and DIG. Altogether, we leverage this model, comprising three labs at the intersection of digital learning and learning analytics, to investigate new things, find pathways to scale, and institutionalize learning.

LESSON 2: UNDERSTANDING FUNDAMENTAL CONDITIONS—THE CENTRALITY OF RELEVANCE

We have an economist colleague who tells us that we worry too much. He says that places like Michigan will always be in business because there are only three places in which young adults finish growing up—college, the military, and prison. He notes that we provide the best return on investment, and he is confident that there will always be parents who want their children to go to Michigan. We think he is both right and profoundly wrong.

Many institutions find themselves confronting serious existential threats. Absent a change to their programs, focus, or delivery, they will not survive in the face of a commoditized curriculum delivered at commodity prices. This is not the case for Michigan. Today we find ourselves with more applicants than ever before and with an entering class that each year exceeds the admission metrics of the class before.

Instead, the challenge that confronts Michigan is one of sustaining disproportionate relevance. In the years following World War II, the United States created federal funding mechanisms that fueled the growth of the research university. Following the arguments laid out in Vannevar Bush's 1945 report to President Truman on the importance of increasing funding for scientific research, research universities have thrived. For half a century, they have been viewed as vital components of an economy based on scientific discovery and technical innovation (Atkinson & Blanpied, 2008). Today, despite compelling evidence of the benefits that have flowed to the nation from that strategy (National Academies, 2007), research universities find themselves increasingly on the periphery. Research is increasingly seen as a luxury at best, and often as an entitlement defended by the academy. Making matters worse, the benefits that should flow from combining research with teaching often fail to materialize, as the two tasks are often seen as competitive with each other.

Fortunately, Michigan, like many other institutions, has seen a renaissance in teaching and learning over the past decade. Gone are the days when faculty were hired and evaluated exclusively on the research part of their portfolios. Teaching clearly matters— whether you judge that by changes to the promotion and tenure process that now require well-documented evidence of teaching as well as research; the number of disciplines that recognize and reward scholarship on teaching the discipline; or the flow of funds into a variety of programs that are designed to enhance learning. But an increased focus on teaching will not be enough. If the University of Michigan is to be as compelling a proposition for the century ahead as it was for the century behind, what happens in the classroom must connect much more directly with the research that happens in the labs, studios, and archives of the university.

Thus, at Michigan we have a vision to redefine public residential education at a 21st-century research university in order to unlock and enable engaged, personalized, and lifelong learning for the entire Michigan community and beyond.

LESSON 3: DISCERNING OUR NORTH STAR—THE PRIMACY OF RESIDENTIAL EDUCATION

At its core, the modern research university is a community bound together by a shared commitment across disciplines to the creation, discovery, analysis, and expression of things the world has not yet seen. This commitment makes the research university different from other forms of higher education. And yet one would be hard pressed to demonstrate the ways in which this commitment infuses the student experience. Research-intensive universities have curricula that remain largely indistinguishable from the curricula of everyone else. They consist mostly of classes sprinkled with opportunities to engage in research. If the curriculum were a dessert, classes would be the cake and research/creation/discovery would be the icing.

At Michigan, we are working to tip the balance. Rather than focusing most of our effort on delivering our curriculum to new audiences, we are concentrating on the ways in which digital technology can be used to enhance the residential experience by focusing on the gifts that physical presence, synchrony, and shared purpose bring to learning. We are exploring ways to use technology to accelerate our students' engagement with research and discovery: ways to deliver introductory material more efficiently so that students can become productive members of research teams early in their tenure; ways to flip classrooms and increase interaction around questions that remain unresolved; ways to extend the communities that form around labs and studios to create a pervasive culture of inquiry; and ways to use data and analytics to create more personalized pathways through the material and the curriculum.

Concretely, this means we are investing in the creation of modular content that can be accessed on demand and reused, in learning analytics that can guide curricular development and individual performance, in developing more gameful approaches to classes, and in a series of discussions with the faculty about the future of the student experience at Michigan.

To be clear, our focus on the residential experience does not mean that we ignore the world of adult learners or global markets. We see opportunities/needs in both of those places. But as we look at those opportunities, we do so grounded in an understanding of the primacy of the residential experience; that understanding fundamentally shapes how we engage other opportunities.

LESSON 4: DON'T MISTAKE BUYING TECHNOLOGY WITH INNOVATION— INNOVATING ON SHARED INFRASTRUCTURE

Although Michigan has tended to take a cautious approach when it comes to investing in online education and the creation of global campuses, we have a long history of investing aggressively in the shared infrastructure that fuels the work of the academy. Michigan was involved deeply in the founding of Internet2, HathiTrust, JStor, and Sakai. We have consistently recognized that shared infrastructure is both scalable and sustainable, and that it allows us to concentrate on using that infrastructure in innovative ways.

Consistent with our history, Michigan is a founding member of the Unizin Consortium for Digital Education. Unizin is designed to provide hosted services (LMSs, content repositories, analytic engines, etc.) in ways that keep the relationships between content, data, and applications "loosely coupled" and available for reuse and analysis. Two principles drive Unizin: first, that universities and their faculty should remain in control of their content, their data, and their reputations/brands; second, that universities thrive when they share infrastructure and compete on what they do with that infrastructure.

The creation of Unizin provides an opportunity for institutions simultaneously to come together and to differentiate themselves. The rising costs of higher education mean that it is not only possible both to collaborate and compete but that it is essential to do both at the same time. In becoming a founding member of Unizin, we joined other partner institutions in a strategic collaborative effort to exert greater control and influence over the digital learning landscape. In parallel, we established the DEI office to scale innovation and to enable strategic decision-making focused on differentiation on top of common infrastructure. We focused finite resources on digital learning initiatives that showcased academic excellence and breadth.

Each of these decisions was intended to differentiate the University of Michigan's approach in an era where disruption is the new normal and change needs to be managed. The digital era impacts all institutions of higher education. But it shouldn't result in a uniform set of actions. We wanted to focus our energy on those strategic choices that would emphasize what is only possible at a great, public, residential research university.

IMAGINING THE FUTURE HIGHER EDUCATION LANDSCAPE

So what does the future of higher education look like? It depends on how institutions, individually and collectively, respond to the emerging conditions. Without intervention, we see a world where state and federal funding continues to fall while the pressure on tuition continues to climb. We see a world where the for-profits continue to work to redefine the public conception of the "well-educated person." If we fail to attend to emerging conditions and fail to focus on differentiating opportunities, we see a not-too-distant future landscape characterized by state universities acting as education warehouses and a small number of well-endowed private institutions catering to the elite. If we fail to respond, we see a world where a narrow focus on competencies and job placement makes college an extension of high school rather than a transformative experience that prepares students for an information-intensive world filled with ambiguity. We fear, in short, the dominance of a commoditized curriculum, a curriculum that better prepares students for the skills of the past century than for a century characterized by near-ubiquitous access to information—a century where knowing what to do with information and how to evaluate it are far more critical than finding it or memorizing it.

On the other hand, if institutions focus on the fundamental conditions and opportunities that shape their institution, if they search for meaningful differentiation, and if they embrace the opportunities that digital technology brings—then the future is bright. The combination of ubiquitous access and networked communities is a change that is surely as profound as Gutenberg's invention of the 15th century. We imagine a world beyond the credit hour, where every student learns from peers as well as the students who came before. We imagine a world that embraces global team teaching, modularity of content, and personalization. We imagine a world where universities strike a balance between serendipitous exploration of a vast set of learning experiences and the predictive impact of an increasingly sophisticated set of personalized learning tools, learning analytics, and digital infrastructure.

James and James no longer occupy separate worlds at either end of campus. We now find ourselves committed to creating a loosely coupled digital ecosystem that allows for the necessary degrees of institutional and individual freedom to take risks and experiment in an emergent world. We now find ourselves organized to investigate new things and find pathways to scale, strengthening linkages between curricular innovation, learning analytics, and digital infrastructure.

A Delicate Balance: Promoting University Change in the 21st Century

Jonathan R. Cole

> *Leadership... is an essentially moral act, not—as in most management—an essentially protective act. It is the assertion of a vision, not simply an exercise of a style: the moral courage to assert a vision of the institution in the future and the intellectual energy to persuade the community or the culture of the wisdom and validity of the vision.*

—A. Bartlett Giamatti (1976, p. 36)

THE NATURE OF THE PROBLEM

Two brief anecdotes should put into perspective the main theme of this essay. The first involves a new president of Columbia University's Teachers College (TC). In an effort to change the direction of the school and to streamline its academic and research programs, the president undertook a yearlong assessment of many existing research centers and institutes at TC. At the end of the year, he announced his decisions to the assembled faculty. After consulting every conceivable constituency, he announced that he had decided to close just one center that had clearly been in a state of cardiac arrest for 30 years or so. When he announced the decision, a rather genteel member of the faculty rose in the back of the grand room and, in his basso profundo voice, said to the president, "Ah, give it a chance!"

The second story involves my own effort while provost at Columbia to close two sclerotic enterprises. It took over a year to shut down a poorly functioning, tiny department and a school, if you can call it that, with four tenured faculty members. Every constituency felt it held veto power over my decision. Nonetheless, the dirty deed was done, and the resources were shifted to efforts that were far more productive. But another year was spent responding to angry letters and emails from faculty, alumni, and others who found what the university had done nothing short of the work of devout Luddites.

The lesson to be taken from all of this is, of course, how too much of a good thing—shared governance—can be transformed into a bad thing, the virtual inability of a university to reorient itself in response to the growth of knowledge. Universities, contrary to popular belief, are highly conservative organizations. And there are good reasons for some degree of resistance to change. But moving these huge tankers in new, uncharted directions has become nearly impossible—with some notable exceptions.

I'm considering here the major research universities in the United States and not most of the 5,000 colleges and universities that make up the multi-tiered and stratified system of higher learning in America. The fundamental problem of choice at research universities has more to do with basic ambiguity over governance than with the ability to articulate alternatives. Who has the authority, beyond the formal authority registered in the statutes or the table of organization, to make such choices? Who has the power to veto the choices made? What are the processes by which the choices of the decision-makers are legitimated with the university community? What is the role of faculty, students, administrative leaders, trustees, and alumni in making such choices? The structure of universities impedes decision-making, creates suspicion among schools and departments about the explicitness and fairness of the criteria for dividing scarce resources, and reduces the flexibility institutions require to respond imaginatively and reasonably to new academic needs and priorities (Cole, 1994).

The resistance to closing any academic unit at a major research university highlights not only the disposition of faculty, students, staff, and loyal alumni to protect everyone's turf lest their own become vulnerable but also the distorted conception of the life cycle of academic departments, specialties, institutes, and centers. We have a marvelous sense of fertilization; we are experts at gestation and early development; we know about maturation and full expansion; but we refuse to confront dying and death. The academic way of death is traditionally through atrophy at a Darwinian pace. We rarely consider the idea of a full life cycle, of what should be associated not only with the beginning but with an end. We have neither the rules that make for orderly governance of choice nor the conceptual frameworks to guide those choices. Moreover, without clear, agreed-upon criteria, many academic leaders, looking at the consequences of boldness among some of their brethren, see, quite accurately, that making significant changes even in the face of limited faculty opposition often leads to larger scale faculty opposition, and potentially to a loss of a leader's authority and legitimacy (Cole, 1994).

Much has been written in this volume about the challenges of dual governance in times of dramatic university change. I will not repeat those arguments or take issue with some proposals here. I will say only that one diagnosis and cure does not fit every stratum or type of university in our complex system. It is abundantly clear that some forms of university governance allow change more easily than others. Still, structural changes will also have to take place at some of the most prestigious universities where long-standing governance structures now seem immutable to change yet inhibit a university where people and ideas can move freely and permeate the borders among departments and schools. It should be no less clear that the roles of trustees have to be articulated with far greater clarity than currently exists at some of our finest public and private universities. We need, as well, to identify bold, courageous, and prudent risk-taking leaders: those who are capable of playing offense as well as defense. Finally, the roles and responsibilities of the academic leaders of a great university relative to its faculty members will also need to be redefined if the institution wishes to create structures that will enable great teaching and research to be done in the 21st century. While the faculty must maintain the principal role in areas such as formulating the curriculum and determining the criteria for selecting undergraduate, graduate, and postdoctoral students, as well as in the hiring, promotion, and tenure of the faculty, there are areas of ambiguity that will need to be clarified if reform is to take place.

Perhaps the most diseased parts of the academic body can be found in organs governing structural change. At the end of the day, some rethinking needs to take place about who is responsible for defending the core values of great universities, most particularly academic freedom and free inquiry, and what mechanisms should be used to decide the dissolution, transformation, and creation of new research or teaching structures at these seats of higher learning.

I turn now to a brief discussion of a few structural reforms internal and external to the university that could allow us to come closer to realizing more fully the potential of our great universities in the 21st century.[12]

---

12 | For a more extensive discussion of these and other changes, see my book *The Great American University: Its Rise to Preeminence, Its Necessary National Role, Why It Must Be Protected* (New York, NY: Public Affairs, 2010) and my forthcoming book *Toward a More Perfect University* (New York, NY: Public Affairs, expected publication January 2016). In the latter book, I address many more changes than space allows me to refer to here.

BUDGETARY REFORM

The most important policy documents at a research university remain its annual operating and capital budgets. In a large number of these houses of intellect, the operating budget alone exceeds $3 billion annually. These are not small enterprises. If you have the capacity to examine budgets closely and understand their nuances, you can get an unusually detailed sense of the academic priorities of the institution. If you follow the money, you will understand better what is going on at these institutions of higher learning. While every large research university needs expert financial and budget officers who are not academics, the key allocation decisions must remain in the hands of academic leaders—generally the president, provost, and deans.

Over the past several decades, most of the great private research universities have moved toward a decentralized budgetary system. This means that revenues generated by the academic units (generally schools) go directly back to those units. This includes, as examples, tuition, gifts, government grants, and student financial aid from outside sources. The central administration then levies a tax on the schools for "common costs," such as facilities charges, library and information technology expenses, and central administrative salaries such as those of the lawyers in the general counsel's office. The tax pays for those offices and their individual members, where it is simply more efficient to have one central office rather than one in every school. The schools are often asked to contribute more than their allocated share of the common costs (arrived at by an algorithm that is generally based to some extent on the size and relative wealth of the unit) so that the central administration has funds to redistribute to its highest priorities. This central tax may be returned, in part or entirely, to the unit that contributes to it, or it may be reallocated to other units. The central administration of the university may have revenues that come from central endowments, intellectual property, and other revenue streams, like indirect costs that come with government and other grants and contracts. It may have endowments that come from gifts to the "center" of the university, but often the center is poor and the schools much "richer." This limits the degrees of freedom for change and reallocation open to the president and provost.

The rationale behind this budgeting structure is that, in principle, it provides incentives for the units to raise revenue and reduce expenditures to yield surpluses that they can keep and reinvest in their academic programs and faculty research efforts. It also has been assumed that placing greater control of resources in the schools enables the university to attract better candidates for deanships, because they will have substantial control (subject to central annual reviews) over their resources. This budgetary system worked reasonably well at many exceptional universities during "the age of silos," or the era of the "multiversity." The open question is whether this form of budgeting has become sufficiently dysfunctional and a drag on the growth of collaborations and the eventual discoveries that come from them to warrant changes in the way resources are allocated. I believe it has.

The fundamental problem with decentralized budgeting is that it tends to create arbitrary borders among schools and disciplines, which often inhibit the cross-fertilization of ideas and collaborative interdisciplinary research and teaching. It tends to weaken the center of the university while strengthening individual units. It also tends to produce academic redundancies. Reallocation of resources becomes immensely difficult. The tail begins to wag the dog. Since each school claims poverty relative to their competitive peer institutions, they resist contributing to the common good of the institution. Inequalities of wealth exist in universities as they do in the larger society, and the rich at universities don't like increased taxes any more than the 1% do in the United States. It all depends on whose ox is gored.

A model that is more centralized would increase easy collaborations across the university and consequently improve the likelihood of important discoveries that are apt to come only from such collaborations. Budgets should not become fetters on the emergence of new ideas. And when the central administration, with appropriate input from faculty groups that help set university priorities, has funds that can be used with greater flexibility, resources can more easily be redistributed to help stimulate new intellectual action. If all tenure billets come back to the provost's office when an individual leaves the university, retires, or dies, the chief academic officer has more discretion and freedom to restructure and reorganize academic units, including increasing or decreasing the number of new faculty members. This centralization offers the possibility of moving forward on new initiatives at a more rapid rate than if tenure and nontenure lines are assumed by tradition to remain in the hands of the departments and schools where they previously had been.

BALANCING TEACHING AND RESEARCH ROLES

Over two decades ago, Derek Bok, then-president of Harvard, warned the academic community about an insidious infection that was eating away at the heart of our great universities: the temptation in efforts to recruit academic stars—the new "free agents"—by offering them lighter teaching loads than other professors (1992). His most recent book, *Higher Education in America* (2013), is still sounding the warning, because the academic community has failed to heed it. On the contrary: Teaching loads have become lighter and lighter. Back in the 1960s, great academic stars, such as the humanists Lionel Trilling and Meyer Schapiro, would be expected typically to teach four or five courses, not two. It did not destroy Columbia or the quality of publications of these exceptional scholars. It was taken as part of the job, and they did not "shop" themselves around in order to minimize their teaching load.[13]

These teaching load changes have had an economic and social impact on great universities. The star professors, using free agency, negotiate higher than normal salaries and require increased research resources while teaching fewer courses. Must we hire two Trillings in order to obtain what we used to get with one? An optimal teaching load properly balances teaching and research. This balance will not be the same in every school or discipline. But I fear that before long, we will have a cadre of research professors who have great prestige and the highest salaries, and who never meet an undergraduate or graduate student other than their own doctoral students and postdoctoral fellows. That would be wrong for the university and the students.

The negotiating ability of academic stars also represents a classic case of a rising tide lifting all boats—and not for the better. After differentiating stars from others, after listening to hostile faculty who are carrying the teaching water, administrations yield to the pressure to move to lower the teaching loads for all members of a department. The general reduction in teaching loads has created a large, disenfranchised, and poorly treated caste, known as *adjunct professors*. This new social class fills the gaps left by the departure of full-time faculty from teaching important courses. Mind you,

---

13 | The sciences have always had lighter teaching loads, in part because productive scientists were expected to support graduate student and postdoctoral research through their research grants and contracts. They spend countless hours writing research proposals for these grants and contracts, which have become increasingly difficult to obtain. This results in their writing multiple proposals in order to support their students and their research.

many adjuncts are exceptional teachers, but they are treated poorly, and reliance on them prevents students at great universities from rubbing minds with the most imaginative and innovative faculty at the university. These adjuncts work for minimal pay and without any of the benefits offered to regular, full-time faculty. The universities ought to work to consolidate these adjunct positions into separate lines of full-time lecturers who may not be tenure-track faculty but who would receive other retirement and health benefits along with living wages, as well as 5-year contracts, which are subject to performance reviews. It is hard to oppose a unionization movement of adjunct faculty when they are treated so shabbily.

Once the genie is out of the bottle, is it possible to get it back in? If it is not, professors ought to be expected to take rather than offer one or two courses a year as part of their professional development and, in an interdisciplinary world, to learn the "new foreign languages." They might also learn and apply new modes of instruction using new technologies. Or they should be required, where qualified, to serve on various truly important committees, such as the undergraduate admissions committee—assuming that they are highly qualified for the task. Faculty members at the great universities work very hard. They are highly self-motivated individuals who seek recognition from their students for excellent teaching, for mentoring postdocs, and for their research discoveries. But there must be structural balance in the system for it to work well, and we, as Derek Bok warned us, are rapidly falling out of balance.

NECESSARY STRUCTURAL REFORM AT THE STATE AND FEDERAL LEVELS FOR THE GREAT PRIVATE AND PUBLIC UNIVERSITIES OF OUR FUTURE

You obviously cannot build or maintain great universities without resources. Over many decades, the great private research universities built up endowments, current-use giving, and federal, state, and private research support, as well as other streams of income, to enable them to use their resources to achieve greatness. The most prestigious state universities were products of many of the same resource streams (and are increasingly so), but with the critical difference that they were dependent on state financing for the education of in-state college and graduate students. Of course, the federal government after World War II played a critical role in creating great discoveries by outsourcing research grants and contracts to universities based on peer review evaluations. If structural changes are needed within our great universities, it is equally important that structural changes take place in the governments that influence the universities' performance and research productivity.

Consider first the necessary changes in the attitudes toward and beliefs about higher education at the highest levels of state governments. Governors and state legislators opine on the value of higher education: We should invest in it; the future of our democratic society depends on education. But the actions of these individuals often contradict their rhetoric. For example, with a paucity of exceptions, states' financing of their universities has simply plummeted over the past several decades. Last year, the *Chronicle of Higher Education* made available an aggregation of data it titled "25 Years of Declining State Support for Public Colleges." Among other things, it showed that state support for dozens of state universities with "very high research activity" (including, for instance, the University of California, Berkeley) had been cut by more than 25% in the past 25 years. When one of the world's great universities, the University of Michigan, receives less than 10% of its total annual operating budget from the state—down from what was once more than 3 times that percentage—then we obtain some idea of what those in political power actually believe. As I've said, look at university budgets and you have a sense of their academic priorities; look at state budgets and you'll get a sense of *those* priorities.

In a fundamental way, many states have violated the trust that was placed in them when they took the land allocated to them by the federal Morrill Act of 1862. Most states sold the land and used the proceeds to build today's land-grant college and university systems.[14] The intent of that act, extended by the second Morrill Act of 1890, was for the states to support these new, important institutions, which today educate about 80% of the nation's undergraduate students. Yet, while in the past they did support students going to college, that support has essentially evaporated. That surely was not the intent of those voting to pass the Morrill Act. Regardless of the other calls on a state's funds (given that they refuse to see higher education as an investment in their future and consequently refuse to raise taxes to finance education), each state's budget for higher education will offer you a sense of how it is valued by its lawmakers. So if great universities are to be held accountable for

---

14 | Also known as the Land Grant Act, the Morrill Act was signed into law by Abraham Lincoln on July 2, 1862. The act gave each state 30,000 acres of public land for each senator and representative, which was based on the census of 1860. The states sold the land, and the proceeds from the sale were used as an endowment fund that would provide support for the colleges in each state. The second Morrill Act of 1890 extended the idea to the former Confederate states and to the historically black colleges. The second act offered the states cash rather than land and was given with the stipulation that race would not be a criterion of admission and that the states would not designate a separate land-grant college for persons of color. In my forthcoming book, I outline a proposal for a new Morrill III Act that would include federal funding for financial aid for new ways of funding high-risk, high-reward research, among other features.

how they spend their money, so should the states that have built universities on funding as a result of the Morrill Act.

States that fail to support their universities with at least 30% of their operating budgets ought to be put on notice by Congress that they can lose federal funding for federal financial aid. They should be given a choice: increase their support of higher learning (while auditing expenses of the universities) or risk the withdrawal of federal funds. In fact, we ought to go still further in terms of structural reorganization. States that lower their support of their public universities and colleges to less than 10% ought to forfeit the right to maintain them as state institutions. Many of our most distinguished state universities have de facto already become quasiprivate or virtually private, although they continue to be forced to operate under their state's education laws. Those institutions should have the option at some threshold level of limited state support (perhaps 3 consecutive years of less than 20% of the budget for financial aid and the cost of faculty and facilities) to declare themselves private universities. This would be called the *opt-out clause* and would be exercised by a vote of an independent Board of Overseers and the academic administration and faculty of the university.

I'm not sure who wins if the state insists that those institutions pay off the cost of the buildings on campus or similar types of state investments. If universities used the present-day value of the funds received from the Morrill Act and subsequent federal support to the universities, it might well be that universities would not have to pay anything for the physical structures (given their depreciation) that have been produced by state, private, and federal funds.

Of course, it would be extremely unfortunate if even one great university had to exercise this option. State universities have a public mission, and to have to abandon that identity would be tragic for aspiring students as well as for the institutions of higher learning that contemplate taking the "poison pill." But the states cannot have it both ways: They cannot castigate the universities for being spendthrifts and ignoring costs while withdrawing their financial support from the universities. It's unlikely, of course, that this proposal could gain much traction in today's Congress. However, even an open discussion and vote on the proposition, or the voting on a single statewide referendum, would shed light on how hypocritical state governments can be in calling simultaneously for universities to teach more students, cut costs, conduct more research, and make progress in the various rankings while simultaneously withdrawing their financial support from those very same institutions of higher learning.

STRUCTURAL REFORMS IN FEDERAL SUPPORT OF HIGHER EDUCATION AND RESEARCH

As critically important as the transmission of knowledge is, the greatness of the American system of higher learning is largely dependent on the innovations, discoveries, and other forms of research conducted within them. Few educated Americans truly understand where world-class research and discoveries come from. In fact, when most educated Americans think of our greatest universities, they think primarily of undergraduate education—a natural tendency among those who really only know about their own experiences at universities or those of their friends and relatives. They don't realize that the laser, FM radio, magnetic resonance imaging, global positioning systems, bar codes, the algorithm for Google, the fetal monitor, the Pap smear, cures for childhood leukemia, the discovery of the insulin gene, the origin of computers, and the origin of biotechnology through the discovery of recombinant DNA all had their origins at our great research universities. Nor are they aware that improved weather forecasting; scientific agriculture; methods of surveying public opinion; and the concepts of *congestion pricing*, *human capital*, and the *self-fulfilling prophecy* were born at our research universities. Even the electric toothbrush, Gatorade, the Heimlich maneuver, and Viagra had their origins at these great universities. Some of these discoveries were a result of serendipity, and some were a result of carefully planned research programs; some of the practical consequences were unanticipated, as in the case of the laser, while others were born with the idea of solving specific practical problems. This was the central message of *The Great American University* (2012).

That research has transformed our lives and the lives of hundreds of millions of people in the world, if not billions. The great transformation in the productivity of the most distinguished universities actually resulted from federal policies toward large-scale, or Big Science, research. That policy was brilliantly outlined in Vannevar Bush's *Science—The Endless Frontier* (1945) and largely implemented after World War II. The compact had many critical elements, not least of which was the outsourcing of research to our universities and the combining of advanced learning with the research enterprise. Another critical element in the compact was that the federal government would *fully* reimburse universities for the actual cost that was spent conducting the research sponsored by the various research arms—not a penny more or less.

Most elements of the compact still work better than similar plans do anywhere else in the world. However, one critical element has been altered in a highly dysfunctional way for both the scientific and scholarly community and for the nation: the way Congress funds science.

Big Science research is costly, but it has big payoffs. It requires some support for faculty members who are the principal investigators on the funded research project, support for facilities and equipment needed for the research, as well as support of postdoctoral fellows and graduate students and technicians who often do the lion's share of the benchwork on these projects while receiving their advanced education. For decades, this compact was largely adhered to. To be sure, there were moments when the government grew suspicious of whether there was value to some of this research. (Remember Wisconsin Senator William Proxmire's "Golden Fleece of the Month Award"?) But the cost of scientific research pales in comparison to the savings on the cost of disease. Stanley Prusiner, the discoverer of prions as a cause of disease, for which he won a Nobel Prize, opines:

> The economics of Alzheimer's do not make sense. We spend nearly $200 billion annually caring for Alzheimer's victims, a colossal sum that includes the lost productivity both of patients and caregivers. Moreover, Alzheimer's victims occupy half of all nursing home beds in America. Yet we devote less than half a billion dollars a year to research, so we spend four hundred times more on care than on research directed at stopping this curse. (2014, p. 255)

The tragedy of all of this is, of course, that we have become less likely to find cures for these diseases and less apt to innovate and make basic discoveries that will fuel our economy for the decades to come. The numbers are stark. According to the recent report of the American Academy of Arts and Sciences Committee on New Models for U.S. Science & Technology Policy, the United States, as of 2013,

> has slipped to tenth place among OECD (Organisation for Economic Co-operation and Development) nations in overall research and development (R&D) investment as a percentage of GDP (gross domestic product)... and continues to fall short of the goal of at least 3 percent adopted by several U.S. presidents. (2014, p. 7)

This disinvestment in science and technology flies in the face of a well-known fact established by the Nobel economist Robert Solow: that scientific and technological advancement is the key to economic growth. It has in fact been the dominant driver of economic growth in the United States over the past 100 years. Unless the federal government can treat investments in science and technology as seed corn that can be harvested profitably by the nation for decades to come, Congress will be responsible for the increasing erosion of one of our nation's claims to greatness.

American ambivalence toward scientific and scholarly expertise has begun to erode aspects of the compact between our preeminent universities and the government policy-makers in Congress. One of the first features of Vannevar Bush's idea for a dominant American presence in postwar science was the full payment of the cost of research, often referred to as *indirect cost recovery* (ICR; this point on full recovery of indirect costs is a major feature of a 2012 report from the National Academy of Sciences titled *Research Universities and the Future of America: Ten Breakthrough Actions Vital to Our Nation's Prosperity and Security*). Over several decades following the war, the level of this reimbursement by the government was a product of negotiation, often so detailed and complex in terms of auditing that the government would have at least one full-time employee permanently located on the university campus to monitor research costs. At the end of the day, the government began to cut back slowly on its reimbursements for audited research expenses. Finally, it put a cap on the reimbursement it would make for facilities charges. In short, by compromising the pact, the federal government was actually making universities pay for government grants and contracts, as well as speculating on the space that would be needed for their future research by building new research structures that, at least in principle, would be filled eventually with research funded by the federal government. Contrary to existing beliefs, both inside and outside the university, research that was in the national interest and was judged to be of high quality in terms of potential discoveries and practical applications was not being fully funded. In short, great research *cost* universities more money than they received for doing it.

This had cascading consequences for our universities. In order to meet the full costs of doing research and of competing for the best researchers (which often required strong economic incentives in the form of state-of-the-art laboratory space and equipment and guaranteed support for a number of postdoctoral students, laboratory technicians, and other support staff), universities had to find dollars within their budgets to cross-subsidize potentially trailblazing research. Two sources were clearly available: tuition dollars from students in the schools of the university and gifts from donors who saw great value in the research. Ironically, some of the increasing cost of tuition for undergraduates, which so often reaches the media and evokes criticism from public officials, including the president of the United States, is a result of the federal government's not living up to the terms of the compact made decades ago.

There are, of course, other ways in which the government has produced unpredictable policies that haunt our finest university research efforts. It is extremely difficult to know what funding increases or cuts will be contained in each federal budget cycle. It is hard to know if restrictions will be placed on the types of work that can be funded, such as stem cell research, or Congress's effort to mandate that the only political science projects to be funded by the National Science Foundation (NSF) must be related to national security issues. In short, it becomes extremely difficult for universities and individual investigators to plan for the longer term. This ought to be rectified. Government policies toward student loans and eligibility for those grants or loans are also ambiguous and often restrictive. In short, the federal government has failed to view university-based research as a form of national defense. It is clearly in the interest of the nation to support both fundamental, curiosity-driven research and research that might lead to effective treatments or cures for diseases. A survey showing that an overwhelming majority of Americans are willing to pay higher taxes to pursue cures for diseases (Research!America, 2007, p. 7) is one example of public attitudes toward supporting research.

Vannevar Bush was trained as an engineer and had the mind of one. But as much as he was an engineer, he was a staunch advocate for basic, fundamental scientific research. He believed in stockpiling basic knowledge and was confident that those fundamental discoveries would lead to new applications downstream that ultimately would create highly skilled jobs and a flourishing national economy. He feared that the support of scientific research would become a political football that would be misused by people who knew little or nothing about scientific research and its effects on the nation. As Congressman Rush Holt, a PhD in physics, observed upon announcing his retirement: The level of scientific discourse

> has not gotten better, let's put it that way. There are still people who read popular science articles, and most members of Congress say they value science and respect scientists. But I don't see more scientific thinking— evidence-based, critical thinking. (Newsmakers, 2014, p. 954)

He was being polite to his colleagues and putting the best face on a serious situation. Foreseeing such a situation, Bush proposed a quasi-independent body, a National Research Foundation that would be given a sum of money and would oversee the conduct of American research. However, neither the Congress nor President Truman were willing to cede control over the purse that supported science and were less than happy about having no say in what was to be studied.

What are some alternative models for the financing of the national research effort in order to stabilize the flow of funds to science? And how can we increase the number of knowledgeable people in charge of the accountability of scientists and their activities? Bush's proposed model was clearly utopian. An alternative structure could be created, however, for making policy decisions and recommending funding decisions and priorities related to knowledge growth. The legislation would not replace any existing agencies that fund science, technology, and innovation that currently exist. Congress could enact the third Morrill Act of, say, 2020, creating a body with some independent funding authority, but a good deal of its effort would be spent on advising Congress on emerging fields, new strategies for conquering disease, and new scholarship that ought to be supported while also advising what the rate of growth in the overall budget ought reasonably to be. This new organizational structure, a National Foundation for Science, Technology, and Scholarship, would act much as the Howard Hughes Medical Institute (HHMI) has functioned in the field of biomedical research: allowing exceptional talent the freedom to work on highly significant problems without the fear of losing their funding. To date, the HHMI program has funded 17 Nobel laureates and more than 170 members of the National Academy of Sciences. The proposed National Foundation for Science, Technology, and Scholarship would also encourage and fund groups of investigators, as HHMI does, "to undertake projects that are new and so large in scope that they require a team with a range of expertise" (Howard Hughes Medical Institute Investigator Program, n.d.).

This body would also provide similar funding opportunities for exceptionally gifted behavioral science researchers and for scholarship of importance in the humanities. Where necessary, it would call on the expertise of people outside of its Board of Governors to assist in assessing the potential and innovativeness of the proposed or ongoing work. Grant recipients would be required to demonstrate progress toward their goal to the foundation's leaders every 3 to 5 years. The foundation's board, along with its advisers, would be "truffle dogs" for younger talent and would try to fund young scientists and innovators with enormous promise and determination. It would also suggest policies to the various federal funding agencies involved in biomedical research on how to lower significantly the age at which younger scientists can establish their own laboratories with RO-1 grants (which today are typically not made until a scientist is at least 40 years old). And like the HHMI, the foundation would put aside some resources to fund extraordinary scientific teaching at the secondary and collegiate levels. These would be honored with prestigious awards that help the nation interest and recruit younger people into science and technology.

In short, we ought to create a quasi-independent, nonpolitical body to oversee science, engineering, behavioral sciences, and the humanities that would recommend a 5-year funding stream for the nation's academic initiatives. This would *not* be an effort at central planning. This would be a group of experts, from the academic community, industry, and other private sectors, who would be selected by the president with majority consent of the Faculty Senate, much as members of the Federal Reserve System are appointed. There would be perhaps seven or nine appointed to the foundation's Board of Governors, who would make final decisions about recommended areas of funding and who would review the progress made in those fields, as well as the efficacy of the peer review system. Once confirmed by the senate, these board members would act as independent agents who view themselves as serving the people of the nation, not any individual or political party.

The objective of the foundation would be to support particularly innovative work on the campuses of the great universities, pay for the full cost of that research, and create what over time would become the largest endowment for science and scholarship in the world. The foundation's various fellows programs would be governed by the same board as the entire foundation but, like the Nobel Prize Committee, there would be an operating portion to the foundation that could not spend more than some small percentage of the fund's total value on actual operations, selection of new fellows, and renewal of continuing fellows while overseeing the quality of the work being done. The board would have both a renowned academic administrator and a director who would report to the Board of Governors.[15]

THE DELICATE BALANCE: A FEW CONCLUSIONS

Let me conclude with a few observations about the relationship between the governance of universities—governance both internal and external to them—and their future greatness. We must recognize that universities contribute to the national welfare in many ways. For the most part, they educate young people who enter the world hopefully prepared to be better citizens than they would have been without their undergraduate training. Universities also ensure that those they educate have skills that are needed in the marketplace and in a more highly technologically driven society. But those graduates should also be significantly better critical thinkers, better analysts of texts, art images, and data, than they would have been without their college education. They should be sufficiently skeptical about the assertions of fact that are thrown at them every day. They must think independently. They must be able to raise new questions for which there are no answers at the back of a textbook.

---

15 | For a more elaborate discussion of this proposal, see my new book *Toward a More Perfect University* (New York, NY: Public Affairs, forthcoming 2016).

To ready young people for today's world thus, we must have universities that are in sync with the world. That world is rapidly changing and rapidly becoming truly international. That means that the structure of our universities that served us so well for the past 75 years will have to change and adapt to new environmental conditions—to a new ecosystem in which these institutions are embedded. They need faculty who have adapted to these new conditions, and they need university leaders who are well positioned to formulate strategic priorities that fit their universities to the world: leaders who are empowered, along with their faculties, to change even the greatest of our universities to accomplish this. The preeminent universities of the United States will not have their walls come tumbling down because of the advance of technology. But technology, whether in the form of massive open online courses (MOOCs) or other innovations, can improve the quality of education for some and bring education to others who would not have access to it otherwise. We must think first of how knowledge is growing; how students are learning; how cognitive and other sciences lead us to understand more than in the past the way we ought to organize work at our seats of higher learning. We need wise, courageous, and imaginative leadership at all levels of our institutions of higher learning to alter the structural forms within universities and the relationships among them in order to maximize their potential.

This may mean transferring to academic administrators some prerogatives that faculty members see as their own and, correlatively, transferring some administrative functions back to the faculty of our most distinguished universities. It will mean having the states and the federal government accept greater responsibility for the support of the teaching and research missions of our universities. All this can be done, but it will be a test of our local and national wills. Passing that test will be crucial for the welfare of our nation and its future.

Key Conclusions | Managing Change

"Managing Change" may seem hubristic, seeking to control what can't be controlled, like Xerxes at the Hellespont ordering the lashing of the waves and chaining of the winds. But managing change that impacts institutions and society as a whole does not mean shackling the whirlwind. It means understanding change and responding to it, seeking opportunities to appropriate and use what is new, to improve what can be reformed and to preserve what must not be lost. Such understandings and responses will differ for different institutions and their different missions, as the authors in this section show.

JAMES HILTON AND JAMES DEVANEY'S KEY CONCLUSIONS:

- Change has its own diversity, and so one challenge is not to overcommit to any one trend, to experiment with innovations that promise returns, and in structures that can be scaled and will allow benefits to be reaped.
- Given a range of real and apparent opportunities among emergent trends, an institution has to be guided in its choices by what makes it distinctive and successful, its "north star."
- An openness to the opportunities technology brings must not be a tendency to confuse technology with innovation, particularly since an institution's differentiating stamp is critical, while technology, especially as promulgated by vendors, is likely to have a homogenizing effect.

JONATHAN R. COLE'S KEY CONCLUSIONS:

- While institutions of higher education, particularly the great research institutions, have helped shape the future, they also cling to the past—to superseded programs, modes of governance, parochialisms, and fiefdoms.
- Infusions of funding are needed, but so is budgetary reform, especially to correct centrifugal dispersal not just of funds but of control and leverage.
- Internal reform needs to be matched by an external, federal recommitment to higher education and especially its research function as a public good, a high-return investment that will support the institutions as they keep pace with and harness change.

The authors in this section, as expansive as their views are, speak primarily to impacts on their kinds of institutions. For the ways in which the ramifications of their views and those of the other authors in this volume may play out over the whole sphere of higher education, see the Afterword.

Afterword: Ramifications

As important as the consequences are for the students, those served by higher education first and foremost, the great index of change may be less what happens to instruction than what happens to instructors. Why not begin with the faculty? After all, teaching innovations must start with those who do the teaching.

The simple answer is that faculty do not change their own working conditions. They respond to them, often resist them, but they do not define them. What has actually defined those working conditions is the same set of circumstances that has put higher education in such a perilous state—above all, decreasing public funding combined with increasing costs (and the increasing need for cost containment).

On the one hand, this has accelerated what Michael Bérubé has called "the adjunctification of the professoriate" (2006, p. 159)—the growing need to make sure the bulk of the teaching is done by underpaid, itinerant, adjunct instructors whose pay is not just far less than the pro-rated equivalent of their full-time counterparts; it is also, by the very nature of part-time status, without the considerable investment in pensions and fringes that institutions of higher education make on behalf of full-time faculty. Whether or not adjunct faculty make a commitment to their own institutions—and many surely do extraordinary work—those institutions have not made a considerable commitment to them.

· But that is only one end of a spectrum of extremes. The other exists as a different reaction to the same conditions. Because the competition for funding, whether for tuition or research, has grown so fierce, conditions for full-time faculty have also changed, re-defining success for them in a way that pulls them still further from the classroom and the lives of their own institutions. Robert Zemsky calls this the "professionalization of the professoriate" after an early analysis of it back in 1985 by the Association of American Colleges in *Integrity in the College Curriculum*:

> Central to the troubles and to the solution are the professors, for the development that overwhelmed the old curriculum and changed the entire nature of higher education was the transformation of the professors from teachers concerned with the characters and minds of their students to professionals, scholars with Ph.D. degrees with an allegiance to academic disciplines stronger than their commitment to teaching or to the life of the institutions where they are employed. (2013, p. 6)

For Zemsky, the de-emphasizing of teaching over research and the allegiance to one's field over one's school became so much more pronounced in the intervening decades that the profession-alization of the professoriate has become nothing less than the "withering of the institutional role in faculty cultures" (2013, p. 26). The marks of success for full-time faculty do not turn on the goals and values of their institutions but on independent projects and self-contained institutes or centers. These are fueled by grants and publications managed by systems of peer review belonging to a universe quite outside the faculty members' own schools. The important gravitational forces pull faculty, especially those who want to be "star" faculty, away from the world of their own institution.

Apparently, higher education has its own variant of the circumstances that define radical income inequality. At one extreme, it has its own 1%: the superstars who have effectively become their own brands in helping to brand their institutions—or in helping to rebrand others when they become players in the academic version of corporate raiding. (Tellingly, a blog called *The Scholarprenuer* recently published a piece called "How to Harness the 'Superstar Effect' in Academia.") When these superstars do teach, it is to high-end graduate students, aspiring future members of the shrinking professoriate they can shape in their own image.

At the opposite extreme, bulking way out of proportion to the elite elect, higher education has a vast cadre of iterant workers and migrant laborers, toiling in the fields for subsistence. These are the ones teaching the preponderance of the crucial introductory courses that define a student's readiness for the rest of his or her college career. Their role is vital, but their reward is meager. The reliance on "temps" for essential services at institutes of higher education far exceeds anything like it in the corporate sphere. It has become, as the title of an *Inside Higher Ed* article put it back in 2007, the "Inexorable March to a Part-Time Faculty."

What are the alternatives to this lopsided scenario, which is not a dystopian future but the present we inhabit? That is what this book has been about: ways of reimagining the status quo, not least of all the role of faculty, as we envision different ways of delivering instruction, deploying instructors, and ensuring effective outcomes. For each re-envisioned role for the faculty in these models, there is a different future for higher education, one that is more or less sustainable, more or less productive.

We can rule one possibility out: There will be no return to the halcyon days when almost all the instruction was done by full-time faculty. There will never be enough funding to buy back the good old days. There may even be reasons to suppose that shouldn't be considered the gold standard. We knew comparatively little of the science or scholarship of learning back then. Assessments were contained within the classroom. Students were at the mercy of their instructors—some of them very good and even life-changing, some forgettable or worse.

Some of us remember those days, but we have already moved far enough beyond them to see the shape of things to come. The outlines emerge in the essays in this volume, but also in the steps taken by a growing number of institutes of higher education in the increasingly stratified and diverse landscape of higher education in the United States. Like the choices of new modes and new business practices, they are the choices confronting those empowered or circumstanced to decide the future of higher education.

REMOTE INSTRUCTION

A number of essays here, above all Michael Zavelle's, have posed the possibility of efficiencies achieved by spending less on teaching that is really, in one way or another, spent on "seats." As the need for physical classrooms attenuates, so of course does the need for physically present instructors (as opposed to digitally present).

Something else happens as well: Because not all instructors are equally adept at online or remote delivery, a new kind of instructor emerges, one adept at instructional design, time management, and asynchronous interaction. Interestingly, this "cyberprof" is likely not to be a professor by the old definition but is much more likely to be an adjunct instructor working at more than one institution, often a practitioner from the field rather than a native inhabitant of higher education.

What you have, then, is instant free agency. In a free market, the especially adept—those with the new skill sets—become more marketable. Demand for them flips the circumstances of the old-fashioned adjunct: Instead of waiting hat in hand for the chance to teach as piecework, they may get to set the terms and, in so doing, set new precedents. This would be especially true for those who teach skills that are more the province of practitioners than of academics. In business fields, in coding and programming, in data analytics and informatics, in health care and cybersecurity, in a hundred emerging high-demand areas that higher education has not kept up with, we have a new kind of instructor: the digitally present free agent.

THE GREAT UNBUNDLING

Back near the turn of the century, James Bess and others began to codify what everyone who has ever taught already sensed. Teaching effectively is not one job; it is many jobs. Bess et al. defined no fewer than eight distinct roles faculty must fill in teaching, including course design, the conveying of content, the managing of discussions, and the assessment of student work. Inevitably, these jobs are being parceled out to members of teams and, in some cases, entirely automated.

We can see the adaptive learning systems described by Candace Thille or the new modes described by Ray Schroeder and Vickie Cook giving compelling form to such possibilities: teaching and learning made more efficacious by getting the best, not from one instructor, but from the right combination of team members and design elements. The goal would be better teaching and learning and so better outcomes, but cost efficiencies might also be achieved.

Carol Twigg began doing cost–benefit analyses of such approaches nearly two decades ago. That these have not been seen as conclusive may have less to do with their efficacy than with the slowness of institutions to commit to decisive change, combined with the rapidity of change within the modes themselves.

STAGING LEARNING

Cathy Davidson makes a compelling argument for how much students can teach one another. They all have unparalleled access to information, so the goal is no longer to give it to them but to get them to apply it—no longer information transfer but information *use*. This was tough to do in the traditional classroom. The complicated logistics and negotiations were daunting; the emphasis on student performance and interaction meant chewing up too much class time; and there was too much fretting among the students over divisions of labor and giving credit where credit is due. But in the realm of digital interaction, this is not just possible but preferable, provided there is the right kind of orchestration. A recent example is her recent course with Bill Kelly as part of the Futures Initiative: the teaching of more than a dozen teachers interacting with their separate classes of their own at nearly that many institutions, all exploring the pedagogical questions posed in the graduate seminar.

This extended experiment points to something George Otte stressed: The full power and potential of new modes and methods are never fully realized when they are first introduced. In this case, we are speaking not just of modes of instruction but modes of discovery. This tiered approach is a reminder that each possibility is really a range of possibilities. The kind of peer interaction central to Cathy Davidson's model can be played out under one teacher—say, in a massive open online course (MOOC)—or managed in teams with "unbundled" roles, such as discussion moderators, graders, and so on. And her own metacourse points to a teaming up that is cross-institutional, that reaches across campuses and even fields. Any of these possibilities would, over time, significantly restructure instruction and the role(s) of faculty.

DISCIPLINARY DISPENSATIONS AND
DIFFERENTIAL DEVELOPMENTS

Some of these approaches work better for some fields than for others. Adaptive learning systems have had their greatest success in fields comprising so-called structured knowledge: areas of teaching and learning where there are right and wrong answers (e.g., math and statistics). "Grayer" fields, where the solutions are more matters of key premises and interpretations (all of the humanities, for instance), are less likely to be helped by mapped progressions and machine grading.

But a far more consequential set of distinctions has less to do with the categorization of knowledge than with the learning time involved. We have been governed by terms and seasons from the start, long before the urbanization (much less the digitalization) of our world. The shared calendar has its conveniences but also its constraints. As students, faculty, and institutions begin to ask what units of time optimize the learning process, the answers are sure to differ by field, by subject, even by instructor and student. The Carnegie unit or credit hour, already under pressure (especially, as Amy Laitinen and others have argued, more as a way of clocking faculty work time than ensuring learning equivalence), is being chipped away by new modes and models as competency-based credit, self-paced instruction, and modularized learning gain more currency and credibility every day.

SO MANY CHOICES, SO LITTLE TIME

The proliferation of possibilities may seem to promise a future where anything is possible. But that is a mirage. Institutions, like curricula, need integrity. An institution's path to its future needs to be just that: a path, not a garden of forking paths. The possible futures posed by new modes and structures create a danger far greater than simply ignoring or resisting change, and that is trying anything and everything. The possible models posed here are not always mutually exclusive, but any institution making too much of too many would be impossible to manage, just as it would be impossible for students to navigate.

Making the right decisions is essential. Here, the essays of Matthew Goldstein, James Hilton and James DeVaney, and Jonathan Cole are key. Each stresses, in different ways, how much of great consequence is included in a small phrase like *making the right decisions*. How they are made, what makes them right, and what they do indeed decide about an institution's future: All these depend on matters that may be specific to a moment or a field, to an institution or a trend among institutions, to a change in technology or society at large. What is right for an institution cannot be measured purely self-referentially; it must take into account the position of that institution in a universe of others making their own decisions—or failing to make them.

Of course, institutions don't make decisions; the people who inhabit them do. And the decision-making process is itself undergoing inexorable change. Some of this is due to changes in what might be called the voter base. "The Graying Professoriate" (the title of a 1999 *Chronicle of Higher Education* survey showing that a third of full-time faculty were over 55) has become "The Shrinking Professoriate" (the title of a 2008 *Inside Higher Ed* piece showing that most full-time jobs in higher education since 2006 have not been faculty jobs). This arguably represents the greatest change of all, more consequential than new methods or technologies. The role of full-time faculty in university leadership is dwindling as their numbers dwindle, and no restoration or reversal will change that. To be sure, many leaders come from their ranks, but allegiances and perspectives shift with the change of roles.

What matters still more is how leadership roles themselves are changing and must change. Institutional change, if not an oxymoron, was always supposed to be slow – until now. The present represents both a sense of exigency and unmistakable evidence of accelerating change. Looming over all, especially the public colleges and universities, are the federal and state governments, increasingly interventionist in their demands of accountability even as they are increasingly parsimonious in their support through funding. Leadership in higher education must confront the realization that decisions may be made for them if they are too dilatory, too reactive rather than proactive. If change itself has changed, becoming the rule rather than the exception, so has decision-making, becoming more necessary and critical than ever before. Decisions must be swift as well as deliberate; leadership must consult yet accept primary responsibility. Being too slow in making a decision is wrong, but only if the decision is right. Changing too little is wrong, but only if the changes are strategic, not centrifugal or diffuse.

Thinking this way can be energizing or paralyzing. The difference turns on seeing a simple truth as complex in its ramifications: Change is the imperative, and effective change will out. What works will ultimately win: It will decide how faculty are deployed, how students are served, how costs are managed. And what works is already before us. Like the changes of the past that turned out to be the important watersheds and turned corners, though not to those who saw them in terms of the status quo, these changes have not shown their full potential or impact. For that to happen, decisions have to be made, ones that blaze the trail for new structures and strategies. Until then, we have to look carefully at what is before us. As William Gibson (1999) said, "The future is already here—it's just not very evenly distributed."

References

THE BIFURCATING HIGHER EDUCATION BUSINESS MODEL

Bowen, W. G. (2013). *Higher education in the digital age.* Princeton, NJ: Princeton University Press.

Dunbar, R. (2010). *How many friends does one person need? Dunbar's number and other evolutionary quirks.* London, England: Faber & Faber.

SHARED GOVERNANCE AND THE NEED FOR DECISIVE ACTION

American Association of University Professors (1940). Statement of principles on academic freedom and tenure. Retrieved from http://www.aaup.org/report/1940-statement-principles-academic-freedom-and-tenure

Creative destruction (2014, June 28). *The Economist.* Retrieved from http://www.economist.com/news/leaders/21605906-cost-crisis-changing-labour-markets-and-new-technology-will-turn-old-institution-its

Kennedy, J. F. (1963, June 25). Address in the Assembly Hall at the Paulskirche in Frankfurt. Retrieved from http://www.presidency.ucsb.edu/ws/?pid=9303

McDonald, M. (2014, April 14). Small U.S. colleges battle death spiral as enrollment drops. *Bloomberg Business*. Retrieved from http://www .bloomberg.com/news/articles/2014-04-14/small-u-s-colleges-battle-death-spiral-as-enrollment-drops

Olson, G. A. (2009, July 23). Exactly what is "shared governance"? *The Chronicle of Higher Education*. Retrieved from http://chronicle.com /article/Exactly-What-Is-Shared/47065/

Rosovsky, H. (2013, September 20.) Research universities: American exceptionalism? The Carnegie Corporation/TIME Summit on Higher Education. Retrieved from http://higheredreporter.carnegie.org /research-universities-american-exceptionalism/

Suster, M. (2013, February 20). In 15 years from now half of US universities may be in bankruptcy. My surprise discussion with @ ClayChristensen. Bothsidesofthetable [Blog post]. Retrieved from http://www.bothsidesofthetable.com/2013/03/03/in-15-years-from-now-half-of-us-universities-may-be-in-bankruptcy-my-surprise-discussion-with-claychristensen/

Taylor, J. B. (2014, September 1). A new twist in online learning at Stanford. *The Wall Street Journal*. Retrieved from http://www .wsj.com/articles/john-taylor-a-new-twist-in-online-learning-at-stanford-1409610594

TECHNOLOGICAL INNOVATION IN EDUCATION: WHAT THE PAST TEACHES, WHAT THE PRESENT PROMISES

Allen, I. E., & Seaman, J. (2003). Sizing the opportunity: The quality and extent of online education in the United States, 2002 and 2003. Needham. MA: The Sloan Consortium. Retrieved from http://olc.onlinelearningconsortium.org/sites/default/files/sizing_opportunity_2.pdf

Allen, I. E., & Seaman, J. (2012). Conflicted: Faculty and online education, 2012. Babson Survey Research Group and Inside Higher Ed. Retrieved from https://www.insidehighered.com/sites/default/server_files/files/IHE-BSRG-Conflict.pdf

Anderson, L. W., & Krathwohl, D. R. (Eds.). (2001). A taxonomy for learning, teaching, and assessing: A revision of Bloom's taxonomy of educational objectives. Boston, MA: Allyn & Bacon.

Bloom, B. S., Engelhart, M. D., Furst, E. J., Hill, W. H., & Krathwohl, D. R. (1956). *Taxonomy of educational objectives: The classification of educational goals.* New York, NY: McKay.

Boyd, D. (2014). *It's complicated: The social lives of networked teens.* New Haven, CT: Yale University Press.

Brooks, D. (2012, May 3). The campus tsunami. *The New York Times.* Retrieved from http://www.nytimes.com/2012/05/04/opinion/brooks-the-campus-tsunami.html

Brown, J. S., & Duguid, P. (2000). *The social life of information.* Cambridge, MA: Harvard Business Press.

Carey, K. (2015). *The end of college: Creating the future of learning and the university of everywhere.* New York, NY: Riverhead Books.

Christensen, C. M., & Horn, M. (2008). *Disrupting class: How disruptive innovation will change the way the world learns.* New York, NY: McGraw-Hill.

Craig, R. (2015). *College disrupted: The great unbundling of higher education.* New York, NY: Palgrave Macmillan.

Crocco, F. (2015). Simulating utopia: Critical simulation and the teaching of utopia. *The Journal of Interactive Technology and Pedagogy, 7.* Retrieved from http://jitp.commons.gc.cuny.edu/simulating-utopia-critical-simulation-and-the-teaching-of-utopia/

Friedman, T. L. (2013, January 26). Revolution hits the universities. *The New York Times.* Retrieved from http://www.nytimes.com/2013/01/27/opinion/sunday/friedman-revolution-hits-the-universities.html

Mapping the futures of higher education (2015). *Newsletter of the Futures Initiative* (Spring 2015 issue). Retrieved from http://futures.gc.cuny.edu/newsletter-spring-2015/

Oblinger, D. (Ed.). (2012). *Game changers: Education and information technologies.* Lawrence, KS: Allen Press.

Pappano, L. (2012, November 2). The year of the MOOC. *The New York Times.* Retrieved from http://www.nytimes.com/2012/11/04/education/edlife/massive-open-online-courses-are-multiplying-at-a-rapid-pace.html

Rogers, E. (1962). *Diffusion of innovations.* New York, NY: Free Press of Glencoe.

Standage, T. (1998). *The Victorian Internet: The remarkable story of the telegraph and the nineteenth century's on-line pioneers.* New York, NY: Berkley Books.

Wray, R. (2002, March 15). First with the message. *The Guardian.* Retrieved from http://www.theguardian.com/business/2002/mar/16/5

Zittrain, J. (2008). *The future of the Internet—and how to stop it.* New Haven, CT: Yale University Press.

CHANGING HIGHER ED FROM THE CLASSROOM UP: HOW THE CONNECTED, PEER-LED CLASSROOM CAN MODEL INSTITUTIONAL TRANSFORMATION

#FutureEd. (2014). *The Chronicle of Higher Education.* Retrieved from http://chronicle.com/blogs/future/

About HASTAC #FutureEd. (2013, May 22). Retrieved from http://www.hastac.org/collections/history-and-future-higher-education

Boyd, D. (2014). *It's complicated: The social lives of networked teens.* New Haven, CT: Yale University Press.

Brady, A., & Konczal, M. (2012). From master plan to no plan: The slow death of public higher education. *Dissent, 59*(4), 10–16.

Brown, J. S. (n.d.). John Seely Brown. Retrieved from http://www.johnseelybrown.com/

Davidson, C., & Goldberg, D. T. (2011). *The future of thinking: Learning institutions in a digital age.* Cambridge, MA: MIT Press.

Davidson, C. et al. (2013). Field notes for twenty-first century literacies. Retrieved from http://www.hastac.org/blogs/cathy-davidson/2013/08/01/chapter-one-how-class-becomes-community-theory-method-examples

Davidson, C., & Ariely, D. (2013). An innovative course on methods and practice of social science and literature, cotaught by Dan Ariely and Cathy N. Davidson, remixed by #DukeSurprise students as a Self-Paced Open Course (SPOC). Retrieved from http://dukesurprise.com/

De Lisi, R. (2002). From marbles to Instant Messenger™: Implications of Piaget's ideas about peer learning. *Theory Into Practice, 41*(1), 5–12.

Dewey, J. (1893). Self-realization as the moral ideal. *The Philosophical Review, 2*(6), 652–664.

Futures Initiative. (n.d.). Retrieved from http://www.gc.cuny.edu/Page-Elements/Academics-Research-Centers-Initiatives/Initiatives-and-Committees/The-Futures-Initiative

Gibson, E. J., & Pick, A. D. (2000). *An ecological approach to perceptual learning and development.* New York, NY: Oxford University Press.

Gibson, J. J. (1977). The theory of affordances. In R. Shaw & J. Bransford (Eds.), *Perceiving, acting, and knowing: Toward an ecological psychology* (pp. 127–143). Hillsdale, NJ: Erlbaum.

Grant, S. (2014). *What counts as learning: Open digital badges for new opportunities.* Irvine, CA: Digital Media and Learning Research Hub. Retrieved from http://dmlhub.net/publications/what-counts-learning

Ito, M., Gutiérrez, K., Livingston, S., Penuel, B., Rhodes, J., Salen, K., Watkins, C. S. (2013). *Connected learning: An agenda for research and design.* Irvine, CA: Digital Media and Learning Research Hub. Retrieved from http://dmlcentral.net/wp-content/uploads/files/connectedlearning_report.pdf

King, A. (2002). Structuring peer interaction to promote high-level cognitive processing. *Theory Into Practice, 41*(1), 33–39.

Losh, E. (2014). *The war on learning: Gaining ground in the digital university.* Cambridge, MA: MIT Press.

MacArthur Foundation Digital Media & Learning Initiative. (n.d.). Retrieved from http://www.macfound.org/programs/learning/

Michael Wesch. Retrieved from https://www.k-state.edu/media/mediaguide/bios/weschbio.html

Mitra, S. (2010, July). The child-driven education. Retrieved from http://www.ted.com/talks/sugata_mitra_the_child_driven_education

Mitra, S. (2013). Hole-in-the-wall. Retrieved from http://hole-in-the-wall.com/index.html

Newfield, C. (forthcoming 2015). *Lowered education: What to do about our downsized future.*

Norman, D. A. (1988). *The psychology of everyday things.* New York, NY: Basic Books.

Rheingold, H. (2012). *Net smart: How to thrive online.* Cambridge, MA: MIT Press.

Selingo, J. (2014, October 29). Demystifying the MOOC. *The New York Times.* Retrieved from http://www.nytimes.com/2014/11/02/education/edlife/demystifying-the-mooc.html

Snow, C. P. (1959). *The two cultures and the scientific revolution.* New York, NY: Cambridge University Press.

Thomas, D., & Brown, J. S. (2011). *A new culture of learning: Cultivating the imagination for a world of constant change.* Lexington, KY: CreateSpace.

Wikistorming. (n.d.). FemTechNet commons. Retrieved from http://femtechnet.newschool.edu/wikistorming/

Zemsky, R. (2013). *Checklist for change: Making American higher education a sustainable enterprise.* New Brunswick, NJ: Rutgers University Press.

WHAT THE SCIENCE OF LEARNING INDICATES WE SHOULD DO DIFFERENTLY

Ambrose, S. A., Bridges, M. W., DiPietro, M., Lovett, M. C., & Norman, M. K. (2010). *How learning works: Seven research-based principles for smart teaching.* San Francisco, CA: Jossey-Bass.

Bajzek, D., Burnette, J., & Rule, G. (2006). Constructing computer models to provide accurate visualizations and authentic online laboratory experiences in an introductory biochemistry course. In G. Richards (Ed.), *Proceedings of the World Conference on E-Learning in Corporate, Government, Healthcare, and Higher Education 2006* (pp. 14–19).

Chesapeake, VA: Association for the Advancement of Computing in Education.

Benassi, V., Overson, C. E., & Hakala, C. (Eds.). (2014). *Applying science of learning in education: Infusing psychological science into the curriculum.* Retrieved from http://teachpsych.org/ebooks/asle2014/index.php

Bowen, W. G., Chingos, M. M., Lack, K. L., & Nygren, T. I. (2012). *Interactive learning online at public universities: Evidence from randomized trials.* New York, NY: ITHAKA.

Budé, L., Imbos, T., van de Wiel, M. W., & Berger, M. P. (2011). The effect of distributed practice on students' conceptual understanding of statistics. *Higher Education, 62,* 69–79.

Cepeda, N. J., Pashler, H., Vul, E., Wixted, J. T., & Rohrer, D. (2006). Distributed practice in verbal recall tasks: A review and quantitative synthesis. *Psychological Bulletin, 132,* 354–380.

Chi, M. T. H. (2005). Common sense conceptions of emergent processes: Why some misconceptions are robust. *Journal of the Learning Sciences, 14,* 161–199.

Clark, R. C., & Mayer, R. E. (2003). *E-learning and the science of instruction.* San Francisco, CA: Wiley.

Clark, R. C., & Mayer, R. E. (2008). *E-learning and the science of instruction* (3rd ed.). San Francisco, CA: Wiley.

delMas, R., Garfield, J., Ooms, A., & Chance, B. (2007). Assessing students' conceptual understanding after a first course in statistics. *Statistics Education Research Journal, 6*(2), 28–58.

diSessa, A. A. (1993). Toward an epistemology of physics. *Cognition and Instruction, 10*(2–3), 105–225.

Dunlosky, J., Rawson, K. A., Marsh, E. J., Nathan, M. J., & Willingham, D. T. (2013). Improving students' learning with effective learning techniques: Promising directions from cognitive and educational psychology. *Psychological Science in the Public Interest, 14*, 4–58.

Kluger, A. N., & DeNisi, A. (1996). The effects of feedback interventions on performance: A historical review, a meta-analysis, and a preliminary feedback intervention theory. *Psychological Bulletin, 119*(2), 254–284.

Koedinger, K. R., Kim, J., Jia, J. Z., McLaughlin, E. A., & Bier, N. B. (2015). Learning is not a spectator sport: Doing is better than watching for learning from a MOOC. In *Proceedings of the 2nd Conference on Learning@Scale (L@S '15)*. Vancouver, British Columbia, Canada.

Lovett, M., Meyer, O., & Thille, C. (2008). The Open Learning Initiative: Measuring the effectiveness of the OLI statistics course in accelerating student learning. *Journal of Interactive Media in Education*. Retrieved from http://jime.open.ac.uk/article/view/2008-14

Mayer, R. E. (2011). *Applying the science of learning.* Boston, MA: Pearson.

Short, J. H. (2000). A counter proposal on evidence-based management. *Frontiers of Health Services Management, 16*(4), 27–34.

WHY NEW MODES ARE NOT NEW BOTTLES FOR OLD WINE

Archives NYU. (2013). Image: Taping a course for Sunrise Semester. Elmer Holmes Bobst Library NYU Archives: New York University. Retrieved from http://www.nyu.edu/library/bobst/research/arch/175/pages/sunrise.htm

Armstrong, P. (2015). Bloom's taxonomy: Original (1956) and revised (2001). Nashville, TN: Center for Learning, Vanderbilt University. Retrieved from http://cft.vanderbilt.edu/guides-sub-pages /blooms-taxonomy/#1956

Bethke, R. (2014, October 17). Why "potential completers" should matter to your institution. *eCampus News*. Retrieved from http://www .ecampusnews.com/top-news/competency-potential-completers -031/

Blaschke, L. M. (2012). Heutagogy and lifelong learning: A review of heutagogical practice and self-determined learning. *The International Review of Research in Open and Distance Learning*, 13(13). Retrieved from http://www.irrodl.org/index.php/irrodl/article /view/1076

Bradt, S. (2014, August 4). The future of MIT education looks more global, modular, and flexible. *MIT News*. Retrieved from http: //newsoffice.mit.edu/2014/future-of-mit-education-0804

Buzbee, L. (2014). *Blackboard: A personal history of the classroom*. Minneapolis, MN: Graywolf Press.

Carr, D. F. (2013, March 11). 12 open educational resources: From Khan to MIT. *InformationWeek*. Retrieved from http://www.informationweek .com/education/online-learning/12-open-educational-resources- from-khan/240150477

Christensen, C. M. (2013, November 1). Innovation imperative: Change everything. *The New York Times*. Retrieved from http: //www.nytimes.com/2013/11/03/education/edlife/online-education- as-an-agent-of-transformation.html

Craig, R. (2014, May 11). Education-as-a-service: 5 ways higher ed must adapt to a changing market. *VentureBeat News*. Retrieved from http://venturebeat.com/2014/05/11/education-as-a-service-5-ways-higher-ed-must-adapt-to-a-changing-market/

Davis, A., & Whalen, M. (2014, November 18). Universities must adapt to evolution of student body. *The Chronicle Herald*. Retrieved from http://thechronicleherald.ca/opinion/1251854-universities-must-adapt-to-evolution-of-student-body

Hecht, I. W. D. (2013). Message 1283: Transformational change: The new face of higher education. *The Department Chair: A Resource for Academic Administrators*, 24(2).

How will the Internet of Everything change education by 2018? (2014, October 13). Internet of Everything [Blog post]. Retrieved from http://www.zdnet.com/how-will-the-internet-of-everything-change-education-by-2018-7000034585/

Johnson, L. A., Becker, S., Estrada, V., & Freeman, A. (2015). *NMC Horizon Report: 2015 Higher Education Edition*. Austin, TX: The New Media Consortium. Retrieved from http://www.nmc.org/publication/nmc-horizon-report-2015-higher-education-edition/

Massachusetts Institute of Technology (MIT). (2014). *Institute-wide task force on the future of MIT education: Final report*. Cambridge, MA: Author. Retrieved from https://future.mit.edu/

Menon, K. (2013, April 22). Robo grader: The future of education? *Dartmouth Undergraduate Journal of Science*. Retrieved from http://

dujs.dartmouth.edu/uncategorized/robo-grader-the-future-of-education#.VZoOaxNVikp

Murray, S. (2014, November 6). Distance learning: Internet opened "Pandora's box" on education. *Business Because*. Retrieved from http://www.businessbecause.com/news/mba-distance-learning/2898/distance-learning-internet-opened-pandoras-box-on-education

Perelman, L. C. (2013). Critique of Mark D. Shermis & Ben Hamner, "Contrasting State-of-the-Art Automated Scoring of Essays: Analysis." *The Journal of Writing Assessment, 6(1)*. Retrieved from http://journalofwritingassessment.org/article.php?article=69

Schroeder, R. (2015). *Student at the center*. Paper presented at the 2015 Illinois Council on Continuing and Higher Education Annual Conference, Chicago, IL. Retrieved from https://sites.google.com/site/studentatcenter/

Vanhemert, K. (2014, November 11). Radical ideas for reinventing college, from Stanford's Design School. *Wired*. Retrieved from http://www.wired.com/2014/11/radical-ideas-reinventing-college-stanfords-design-school/

Weise, M. (2014, October 17). The real revolution in online education isn't MOOCs. *Harvard Business Review*. Retrieved from https://hbr.org/2014/10/the-real-revolution-in-online-education-isnt-moocs/

Weise, M. R., & Christensen, C. M. (2014). *Hire education: Mastery, modularization, and the workforce revolution*. San Francisco, CA: Clayton Christensen Institute for Disruptive Innovation.

STRATEGIC DECISION-MAKING IN AN EMERGENT WORLD

Atkinson, R. C., & Blanpied, W. A. (2008). Research universities: Core of the U.S. science and technology system. *Technology in Society, 30,* 30–48.

Borland, J. (2000, September 8). Metallica, Dr. Dre urge colleges to cut Napster access. *CNET.* Retrieved from http://www.cnet.com/news/metallica-dr-dre-urge-colleges-to-cut-napster-access/

Brown, J., & Hagel, J. (2003, June) Does IT matter? An HBR debate. *Harvard Business Review* (2003), 2–4.

Carr, N. G. (2003, May). IT doesn't matter. *Harvard Business Review, 81,* 41–49.

Dr. Dre (1992). *The Chronic.* Death Row Records.

Goldman, D. (2010, February 3.) Music's lost decade: Sales cut in half. *CNN Money.* Retrieved from http://money.cnn.com/2010/02/02/news/companies/napster_music_industry/

González, J. (2012, June 6). Certificates rise to 22% of postsecondary credentials awarded, report says. *Chronicle of Higher Education.* Retrieved from http://chronicle.com/article/Certificates-Rise-to-22-of/132143/

Gurin, P., Nagda, B. A., & Lopez, G. E. (2004). The benefits of diversity in education for democratic citizenship. *Journal of Social Issues, 60,* 17–34.

Hilton, J. L. (2014, September 15). Enter Unizin. *EDUCAUSE Review, 49*(5), 104–105.

Holland, J. H. (2006). Studying complex adaptive systems. *Journal of System Science and Complexity, 19*, 1–8.

Naughton, J. (2012). *From Gutenberg to Zuckerberg: Disruptive innovation in the age of the Internet.* New York, NY: Quercus.

Rising above the gathering storm: Energizing and employing America for a brighter economic future (2007). Washington, DC: National Academies Press.

Wikinvest (2015). Market capitalization for Apple 1999/2008. Retrieved from http://www.wikinvest.com/stock/Apple_%28AAPL%29/Data/Market_Capitalization/1999

A DELICATE BALANCE: PROMOTING UNIVERSITY CHANGE IN THE 21ST CENTURY

25 years of declining state support for public colleges. (2014, March 3). *The Chronicle of Higher Education.* Retrieved from http://chronicle.com/article/25-Years-of-Declining-State/144973

American Academy of Arts and Sciences Committee on New Models for U.S. Science & Technology Policy (2014). *Restoring the foundation: The vital role of research in preserving the American dream.* Cambridge, MA: American Academy of Arts and Sciences.

Bok, D. (1992). Reclaiming the public trust. *Change, 24*(4), 12–19.

Bok, D. (2013). *Higher education in America.* Princeton, NJ: Princeton University Press.

Bush, V. (1945). *Science: The endless frontier—A report to the President.* Washington, DC: U.S. Government Printing Office. Retrieved from http://www.nsf.gov/about/history/vbush1945.htm

Cole, J. R. (1994). Dilemmas of choice facing research universities. In J. R. Cole, E. G. Barber, & S. R. Graubard (Eds.), *The research university in a time of discontent* (1-36). Baltimore, MD: Johns Hopkins University Press.

Cole, J. R. (2009). *The great American university: Its rise to preeminence, its indispensable national role, why it must be protected.* New York, NY: Public Affairs.

Giamatti, A. B. (1976). *A free and ordered space: The real world of the university.* New York, NY: W. W. Norton.

Howard Hughes Medical Institute Investigator Program (n.d.). Retrieved from http://www.hhmi.org/programs/biomedical-research/investigator-program

National Academy of Sciences (2012). *Research universities and the future of America: Ten breakthrough actions vital to our nation's prosperity and security.* Washington, DC: National Academies Press.

Newsmakers (2014, February 28). *Science, 343,* 954–955.

Prusiner, S. B. (2014). *Madness and discovery: The discovery of prions—A new biological principle of disease.* New Haven, CT: Yale University Press.

Research!America (2007). *America speaks* (Vol. 8). Retrieved from http://www.researchamerica.org/sites/default/files/AmericaSpeaks V8.pdf

Solow, R. (1956). A contribution to the theory of economic growth. *Quarterly Journal of Economics, 70,* 65–94.

Solow, R. (1957). Technical change and the aggregate production function. *Review of Economics and Statistics, 39,* 312–320.

AFTERWORD: RAMIFICATIONS

Association of American Colleges. (1985). *Integrity in the college curriculum: A report to the academic community.* Washington, DC: Author.

Bérubé, M. (2006). *Rhetorical occasions: Essays on humans and the humanities.* Chapel Hill: University of North Carolina Press.

Bess, J. (2000). *Teaching alone, teaching together: Transforming the structure of teams for teaching.* San Francisco, CA: Jossey-Bass.

The Futures Initiative. (2015). Retrieved from http://www.gc.cuny.edu/Page-Elements/Academics-Research-Centers-Initiatives/Initiatives-and-Committees/The-Futures-Initiative

Gibson, W. (1999, November 30). The science in science fiction. On *Talk of the Nation,* NPR (Timecode 11:55). Retrieved from http://www.npr.org/templates/story/story.php?storyId=1067220

Jaschik, S. (2008, March 12). The shrinking professoriate. *Inside Higher Ed.* Retrieved from https://www.insidehighered.com/news/2008/03/12/jobs

Laitinen, A. (2012). *Cracking the credit hour.* Washington, DC: New America Foundation.

Lederman, D. (2007, March 28). Inexorable march to a part-time faculty. *Inside Higher Ed*. Retrieved from https://www.insidehighered.com/news/2007/03/28/faculty

Magner, D. K. (1999, September 3). The graying professoriate. *The Chronicle of Higher Education*. Retrieved from https://chroniclecareers.com/article/The-Graying-Professoriate/27612/

Rank, S. (2015). How to harness the "superstar effect" in academia. The Scholarprenuer [Blog post]. Retrieved from http://thescholarpreneur.com/harness-superstar-effect-academia/

Twigg, C. A. (1999). *Improving learning & reducing costs: Redesigning large-enrollment courses*. Saratoga Springs, NY: National Center for Academic Transformation. Retrieved from http://www.thencat.org/Monographs/ImpLearn.html

Zemsky, R. (2013). *Checklist for change: Making American higher education a sustainable enterprise*. New Brunswick, NJ: Rutgers University Press.

Contributors

JONATHAN R. COLE is the John Mitchell Mason Professor of Columbia University and was its provost and dean of faculties from 1989 to 2003. Since his term as provost he has focused much of his scholarly attention on issues facing higher education. His recent books on that subject include *The Great American University: Its Rise to Preeminence, Its Indispensable National Role, Why It Must Be Protected* (2011) and *Toward a More Perfect University* (2016); and he co-edited and contributed to two volumes of essays, *Who's Afraid of Academic Freedom?* (2015), and *The Research University in a Time of Discontent* (1994). He also has published books and articles in the sociology of science. He is a member of the American Academy of Arts and Sciences, the American Philosophical Society, and the Council on Foreign Relations. He is a member of many university and non-profit boards of trustees. He lives in New York.

VICKIE COOK is the Director of the Center for Online Learning, Research and Service (COLRS) and Associate Research Professor in the College of Education at the University of Illinois Springfield. Dr. Cook has been actively engaged providing consulting and faculty development with educational leaders across the U.S. and in Mexico. Her work has been published in a variety of national educational publications including part of the team, which authored the UPCEA

Hallmarks of Excellence. She teaches online in the Teaching English as a Second Language concentration of the Masters of Arts in Education program at University of Illinois Springfield. Her current research agenda focuses on two areas. First, exploring mobile learning through a heutagogical lens and also the impact of a systems approach for online leadership.

CATHY N. DAVIDSON is Distinguished Professor in the PhD Program in English at the Graduate Center, The City University of New York, and Director of the Futures Initiative. She has published more than twenty books, most recently *Now You See It: How the Brain Science of Attention Will Transform the Way We Live, Work, and Learn*. Previously, Davidson had a long career at Duke University where she held two distinguished chairs and served, from 1998–2006, as Duke's (and the nation's) first Vice Provost of Interdisciplinary Studies. In 2002, she cofounded the Humanities, Arts, Science, and Technology Alliance and Collaboratory (hastac.org), the world's first academic social network, now with 13,000+ members. She co-directs the Digital Media and Learning Competitions, supported by the John D. and Catherine T. MacArthur Foundation. In 2011, President Obama appointed her to the National Council on the Humanities. She is the first educator on the Board of Directors of Mozilla and is the 2015 recipient of the Ernest L. Boyer Award for "significant contributions to American higher education" given by the New American Colleges and University.

JAMES DEVANEY is the Associate Vice Provost for Digital Education and Innovation at the University of Michigan, where he leads the Office of Digital Education & Innovation including its Academic

Innovation Fund as well as three labs operating at the intersection of digital learning and learning analytics. Prior to his role at U-M, James was a senior director at Huron Consulting Group where he co-founded the firm's Global Education and Digital Education practices. Previously, he lived in the United Arab Emirates where he established the firm's presence in the MENA region. James has worked with more than 50 universities in 15 countries across the Middle East, North Africa, Europe, Australia, and North America. In addition to world-class research universities, James has worked with startup colleges and universities, new educational ventures and international branch campuses, national libraries, museums, K-12 focused nonprofits, think tanks, and other social enterprise organizations.

MATTHEW GOLDSTEIN served as Chancellor of The City University of New York for fourteen years until 2013, the first CUNY graduate to lead the nation's largest urban public university. During that time the University saw a resurgence in growth, in quality indicators, economic stability and reputation. Prior to serving as chancellor, Dr. Goldstein held senior academic and administrative positions, including President of Adelphi University, President of Baruch College, President of the Research Foundation, and CUNY's Acting Vice Chancellor for Academic Affairs. He is the author of numerous research papers in mathematics and co-author of three advanced books on statistics. He was awarded the Carnegie Academic Leadership Award in 2007 and elected a Fellow of the American Academy of Arts and Sciences in 2006, among many other honors. Currently, Dr. Goldstein is chair of the Board of Trustees of the JP Morgan Funds and a member of the Executive Committee of the Business–Higher Education Forum.

JAMES HILTON is University Librarian and Dean of Libraries and Vice Provost for Digital Education and Innovation at the University of Michigan, where he leads one of the world's largest and most innovative library systems, and spearheads the development of campus-wide strategies, policies and programs around educational technology. He is also Arthur F. Thurnau Professor in the School of Information. A national leader in technology issues around higher education, he has led, championed and fostered technology initiatives that cross boundaries between institutions, and between academic and information technology units. He began his career as a faculty member in the University of Michigan's Department of Psychology, where he was three-time recipient of the Excellence in Education Award, served as the Chair of Undergraduate Studies between 1991 and 2000, and was awarded the Class of 1923 Memorial Teaching Award.

GEORGE OTTE was named Director of Instructional Technology for The City University of New York in 2001, and renamed the University Director of Academic Technology in 2008. That same year he became the chief academic officer of the CUNY School of Professional Studies, home of CUNY's fully online degrees. (He was there for the launch of the first online degree; there are now twelve; eight bachelor's and four master's.) An English professor for decades—he directed writing programs at Baruch College for fifteen years and was awarded that school's Teaching Excellence award in 1993—he is on the doctoral faculty of the programs in English, Urban Education, and Interactive Technology and Pedagogy at the CUNY Graduate Center. He has chaired the CUNY IT Conference since 2002 and the CUNY Committee on Academic Technology since 2008. He earned his doctorate at Stanford in what was then the new (still extant) Modern Thought and Literature program in 1982.

RAY SCHROEDER is Professor Emeritus, Associate Vice Chancellor for Online Learning at the University of Illinois Springfield and Director of the Center for Online Leadership at the University Continuing and Professional Education Association (UPCEA). Each year, Schroeder publishes and presents nationally in online and technology-enhanced learning. Ray publishes five daily blogs on various aspects of news, research, and trends in technology-enhanced learning in higher education. He is recipient of the 2002 Sloan-C award for the Most Outstanding Achievement in Online Learning by an Individual, University of Southern Maine "Visiting Scholar in Online Learning" 2006–2009 and inaugural 2010 recipient of the Sloan Consortium's highest individual award—the A. Frank Mayadas Leadership Award. Ray received the 2011 University of Illinois Distinguished Service Award. He is an inaugural Sloan Consortium Fellow and the 2012 Innovation Fellow for Digital Learning by the UPCEA.

CANDACE THILLE is the founding director of the Open Learning Initiative (OLI) at Carnegie Mellon University and at Stanford University and an assistant professor in the Graduate School of Education at Stanford University. Her focus is in applying research results to the design of open web-based learning environments and in using those environments to conduct research in human learning. Dr. Thille serves on the board of the Association of American Colleges and Universities; on the Assessment 2020 Task Force of the American Board of Internal Medicine; on the advisory council for the Association of American Universities STEM initiative; on the advisory council for the NSF Directorate for EHR. She served on the working group of the President's Council of Advisors on Science and Technology that produced the Engage to Excel report and on the U.S. Department of Education working group, co-authoring The 2010 National Education Technology Plan.

MICHAEL ZAVELLE is the Chief Financial Strategist for the New Mexico Finance Authority responsible for NMFA's and NMDOT's bond programs including issuance, investor relations, portfolio strategy and modeling. His background in college administration includes service as Vice Chancellor for Academic Administration & Planning for City University of New York and in chief financial and business officer positions for Fisk University, Brooklyn College, and Baruch College. His financial models changed CUNY resource allocation methodology. As the Senior Vice President/COO for the New York Public Library, Mr. Zavelle developed the financial models and was the inaugural President of the Research Collections and Preservation Consortium (ReCAP) formed with Princeton and Columbia Universities. Mr. Zavelle spent nine years in Asia as a Managing Director with Chase Manhattan Asia Limited in Hong Kong and Tokyo. His BA in economics is from Dartmouth College and his MBA is from Harvard University.

Index

A

AAU (Association of American Universities), 10

academic professional associations, 83–85

academics. *see* faculty

accelerated learning study, 100–102

accessibility attribute, 67

accountability, 2, 40–41, 45. *see also* faculty; trustees

acknowledged responsibility, 4

active learning. *see* peer learning

adaptability attribute, 67

adaptive learning systems, 3, 189

Adelphi University, 34

adjunct professors, 22, 166–167, 183–184

adoption patterns, 95

affiliations, 48

affordability. *see* costs

Affordable Colleges Online, 9–10

affordances, 75–77

Allen, I. Elaine, 65

American Academy of Arts and Sciences Committee, 173

Apple, 139–140

Ariely, Dan, 81–82

Arizona State University (ASU), 9

Association of American Universities (AAU), 10

asynchronous online courses, 24–25

B

Babbage, Charles, 57

bachelor's degrees, 2, 9, 10, 35, 118, 143

Bady, Aaron, 92

Balsamo, Anne, 89

BASIC computer language, 7–8

Bean, Martin, 119

Beethoven's String Quartet metaphor, 13

Bell, Alexander Graham, 61–62

beneficial learning model, 16–18

Bérubé, Michael, 183–184

Bess, James, 187

billionaires, 46–47

blackboards, 115

Blatecky, Alan, 84

Bloom's taxonomy, 68, 122–23, 131

board members, 34, 178

board of trustees. *see* trustees

Bok, Derek, 165

Bowen, William G., 11–12, 13, 100

Boyd, Danah, 60, 76

brands, 46, 185

brandy invention, 56

Brown, John Seely, 64–65, 84

budgets, 163–165, 182

Bush, Vannevar, 172, 174, 176, 177

business models, 7. *see also* Fannies in the Seats (FITS) business model; Model A-1; Model X